Best wishes –
To your Loyes –

Dale Russell

Hell Above Deep Water Below

Dale Russell

Copyright © 1995
by Dale Russell

Russell, Dale, 1924-
Hell above, deep water below / Dale Russell.
p. cm.
Includes bibliographical references and index.
Preassigned LCCN: 94-073166
ISBN 0-9643849-9-X

1. Flying Fish (Submarine) 2. World War, 1939-1945--Naval
operations--Submarine--Personal narratives. 3. World War
1939-1945--Naval operations, American--Personal narratives.
4. Russell, Dale, 1924- I. Title

D783.5.F59 1995   940.54'5973
                                   QBI94-21153

Published by: Bayocean Enterprises
               6950 Bayocean Road
               Tillamook, OR 97141

Cover art by: Clive Davies

Design and Production by: Frontier Publishing
                 Seaside, OR 97138

Printed in the United States of America

Dedication

TO ALL SUBMARINERS:

past, present, and future.

Preface

Although this is a story about my World War II experiences and the exploits of one submarine during the time I served on her, it is intended to be more than that. I have tried to capture the moods of a fighting ship's crew, caught up in the momentum of "war fever."

Unlike most submarine stories, which have been authored by a former high-ranking Naval officer, this one is written by a former "white hat" sailor, a Third Class Torpedoman. As such, I am not bound by protocol. All the writing is as accurate as revived memory and limited research could make it.

Robert A. Harding, "Stretch" and Roberts are the only fictitious names used, but the incidents in which they are presented are factual. I chose to use these two fictitious names to avoid possible embarrassment to friends and former shipmates, even though I do not consider their behavior to have been anything except normal, colorful, and honorable.

I have tried to recreate the actual battle scenes, which contrast the horror and the light moments of submarine warfare. I have also made an honest effort to keep the story in a neutral vein, and purposely tried not to glorify World War II, or my part in it. I have written the facts as I saw them, and as I now see them in my mind's eye.

During, before, and after World War II, little information was released about submarine activity. This is still true today. A submarine usually operates alone in enemy waters. For safety and success, the nature of submarine warfare mandates secretive operations. From the quiet manner in which the submarine operates, to the lack of information released to the public, the name SILENT SERVICE was and still is fitting.

Some readers may be troubled by the many references to the consumption of alcoholic beverages. That was not an unusual occurrence in our armed forces during that war. I ask those readers to recognize the circumstances related to war, as well as the periods during which those incidents took place. During those times values were warped and inhibitions could easily be pushed aside. For at least a short time the mind could be numbed. Tomorrow was an uncertain word for many people.

I ask the reader to understand that I used the word "Jap" and other derogatory terms as a seeming necessity. I felt that it was important for the language and attitudes of that period to be recreated honestly.

Veterans of World War II, on both sides of that conflict, are not the same people as those young men and women were during the war. These many years have passed, memories have faded, wounds have healed, hatreds have died, but to some extent, the demons of war still remain in our minds.

Acknowledgments

During the first and second *Flying Fish* reunions, 1991 and 1993, many of my former shipmates helped me revive memories of the World War II years. The information gained during our discussions gave me freedom from doubt, knowing that the book I was planning would be as accurate as the span of time, collective memories, limited research, and my writing ability could make it.

To the best of my knowledge, with the exception of the torpedo photograph, and that of our ship's photographer coming on deck through the hatch, all others were taken by that photographer, Francis R. Birkner. After printing multiple copies of the non-classified pictures, "Dick" distributed them to his shipmates.

A special thanks to those shipmates and to Kay Birkner, widow of "Dick," whose photographs, combined with those I had, make up the picture presentation.

I also thank Mark V. Lynsky for the article from the *Honolulu Star-Bulletin.*

With appreciation, I recognize Ann Beckwith's suggestions, encouragement, and contribution to the cover flaps.

Dale Russell

Table of Contents

Photographs and Illustrations

Introduction

America was still war-weary. It was a mere 23 years since she and her Allies had won the bloody, four-year, World War I, the war which was supposed to have been the war to end all major wars.

In the thinking of many, the weapons were so sophisticated and destructive that no nation's leaders would ever chance another war. The lesson didn't take. Now America and the world were confronted with new, and perhaps more dangerous enemies.

Most college and high school students had relatives who fought in the previous war, but most of their American history textbooks devoted just one chapter to it. Perhaps the educational establishments of other nations also treated that war too lightly. Whatever the reasons, lessons on the terrible consequences of war were not learned.

Other things of serious concern had taken place in our country since the end of World War I. Our people were looking inward and trying to pull themselves out of the Great Depression. Our factories were slow at converting to peacetime production. Money was scarce and the demand for new products was not there.

While our country tried to maintain a non-warlike

attitude, Japan, which had not been directly involved in World War I, was building its war machines and putting them into use. When Japan began to move against her neighbors, we looked the other way. It was still a big world and things which occurred on the other side of it, seemed too far away to cause most Americans concern. There were no televisions to bring the visual atrocities to the eyes of our people. Newspaper and radio reportings were minimal.

Japan, for years, had widespread poverty and perhaps the "pastures looked greener on the other side of the fence." She became a very militaristic nation.

In the latter part of the last century and in the early part of our present century, Japan acquired many of the small Pacific islands. With the annexation of Korea in 1910, her movement against Manchuria in 1931, her five-year war with China and the acquisition of Shanghai in 1937, her imperialistic bent should have been a warning to all the world. She was soon to turn her attention and intentions towards greater acquisitions in the Pacific, south and southeast of her home islands.

The December 7, 1941, destructive attack on the American warships in Pearl Harbor gave the Japanese virtual control over the Pacific Ocean. The U.S. Naval Surface Fleet needed time for repair and rebuilding. There were no rockets to carry the war to the Japanese, and there were no long-range planes capable of securing the waters which the enemy seemed to dominate. How would America hold back the enemy? The need was obvious and the task imperative. The responsibility was placed upon the Silent Service, a group of select men and their unique ships, the submarines.

The offensive weapon was readied, and a protective shield was effected. The odds were great and the price paid was high. The war-years mortality rate on the fighting submarines was greater than 20 percent. But these committed vessels stood as a barrier between the Japanese Navy and our vulnerable waters in the early stages of the war. They continued to take a heavy toll on Japanese war ships and merchant vessels throughout the war years. Submariners, making up less than two percent of our naval forces, destroyed 50 percent of the Japanese merchant ships and 34 percent of their war ships.

About the Author

The author's life exemplifies the typical adventurous spirit of the submariner. He has always sought challenges in a variety of forms, which include: boxing, motorcycle riding, breaking horses, and alpine ski racing. An avid lover of nature, he has backpacked on many wilderness trails and hiked into secluded fishing areas.

These activities served to spice up his life while he devoted twenty-two years to high school classroom teaching and seven years to school administration.

In 1949, he received a Bachelor of Science degree from the University of Mansfield, Mansfield, Pennsylvania. In 1952, he gained a Master of Arts degree from the University of Denver, Denver, Colorado. In quest of specific knowledge, he has studied at the University of Nevada - Reno, Oregon State University, Portland State University, and the University of Oregon.

During his years in the field of education, his love of nature and spirit of adventure led him to still another demanding sport — mountain and rock climbing. He has climbed in the Rocky Mountains, the Cascade Mountain Range, and the California and Nevada High Sierras. His enthusiasm for the sport took him to the Alps and the summits of the Matterhorn and Mount Blanc.

During his years of serious climbing, he was a certified climb leader with the Mazamas. This century-old climbing club, based in Portland, Oregon, has nearly 3,000 members.

He has shared many of his climbing experiences between 1982 and 1990 in *For Love of Mountains*, a desktop publication which is used as a reference book by many local climbers.

After World War II, the author didn't join any veterans' organizations.He put all of his war experiences behind him. Since he did not discuss these war experiences, they remained locked in his mind, unaltered. The first *Flying Fish* reunion was held in October of 1991. The recollection of memories, and the sharing of them with shipmates, led to the writing of *Hell Above, Deep Water Below.*

Anatomy of a Submarine

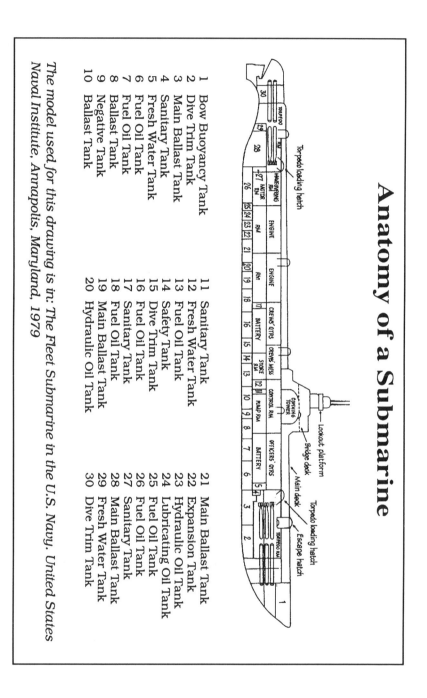

1 Bow Buoyancy Tank
2 Dive Trim Tank
3 Main Ballast Tank
4 Sanitary Tank
5 Fresh Water Tank
6 Fuel Oil Tank
7 Fuel Oil Tank
8 Ballast Tank
9 Negative Tank
10 Ballast Tank

11 Sanitary Tank
12 Fresh Water Tank
13 Fuel Oil Tank
14 Safety Tank
15 Dive Trim Tank
16 Fuel Oil Tank
17 Sanitary Tank
18 Fuel Oil Tank
19 Main Ballast Tank
20 Hydraulic Oil Tank

21 Main Ballast Tank
22 Expansion Tank
23 Hydraulic Oil Tank
24 Lubricating Oil Tank
25 Fuel Oil Tank
26 Fuel Oil Tank
27 Sanitary Tank
28 Main Ballast Tank
29 Fresh Water Tank
30 Dive Trim Tank

The model used for this drawing is in: The Fleet Submarine in the U.S. Navy. United States Naval Institute, Annapolis, Maryland, 1979

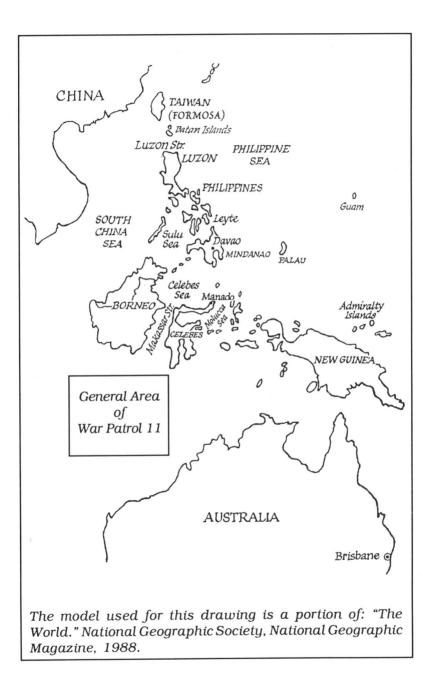

CHINA

TAIWAN
(FORMOSA)
Batan Islands

Luzon Str.

LUZON

PHILIPPINE
SEA

PHILIPPINES

SOUTH
CHINA
SEA

Sulu
Sea

Leyte

Davao

MINDANAO

PALAU

Guam

Celebes
Sea

Manado

BORNEO

CELEBES

Molucca
Sea

Makassar Str.

Admiralty
Islands

NEW GUINEA

General Area
of
War Patrol 11

AUSTRALIA

Brisbane

The model used for this drawing is a portion of: "The World." National Geographic Society, National Geographic Magazine, 1988.

Upper Left:
Raymond D. Sproull

Lower Left:
Edward P. Schoonmaker

Below:
John W. Mattingly

Chapter *1*

Depth Charge Attack

Night after day, the *Flying Fish* slowly cruised through the waters of a quiet Pacific Ocean, navigated by compass and chart. A radarman constantly scanned the waters in all directions. Lookouts were alert. Radar could not detect a periscope or a torpedo wake, and we all realized that radar could not always be trusted. The radarman and lookouts knew that their lives and those of the entire crew could depend upon their diligence.

It was the first week in August, 1944. The *Flying Fish*, no stranger to war, was making her 11th war patrol; I was experiencing my first.

Most of our patrolling was south and east of the Davao Gulf and in the shipping lanes between Davao and Palau, with much effort and time concentrated on the gulf. We had 24 torpedoes to deliver and shipping lanes were always protected. We were hunting and being hunted: the purpose and fate of a fighting submarine.

Below deck, a duty crew was standing by to spring into action if necessary. Normal routine tasks were attended to. Batteries, necessary for the entire electrical system, which included the ship's propulsion when submerged, were periodically checked. Trained

1

ears monitored the engines and minor adjustments were made. In a seemingly almost casual way, all systems were constantly being evaluated. Although there was time for semi-relaxation with reading or card games, all members of the crew were constantly alert.

We were in a war zone, in enemy waters, nothing could be left to chance. Our orders were to intercept and sink any worthwhile ship. Anything we encountered would belong to the enemy.

In our search for suitable targets we worked the shoreline, often very near harbor outlets, when water depth was adequate. One busy and ostensibly prosperous port city looked especially promising to Commander Risser when he observed a great amount of vehicular activity on a road near the beach, seemingly heading to and from the port. This could mean the exit of loaded ships in a day or two. The observations were made through the periscope with the *Flying Fish* at a depth of 68 feet. During the hours of darkness, we moved a greater distance offshore and stayed on the surface as much as possible. On the surface, we had radar as well as lookouts making observations, searching for targets or danger. Powered by diesel engines, we covered a greater area, had the speed to move into a position to intercept a possible target, and could keep our batteries fully charged. Any of the four engines could be used to turn the battery-charging generators.

We worked the area for three days and nights, but the expected freighter or freighters did not appear. Traffic to and from the port should have included other targets and did, but none were worthy of torpedo expenditure. These smaller vessels were tempting gunfire targets; however, that type of action would not have been prudent. Japanese search planes patrolled the coastline constantly. While patrolling another area, we were forced to dive several times by threatening planes. Once, depth bombs were dropped near us after we had dived.

(Depth bombs, except for shape, were similar to depth charges in that they both had pressure mechanisms which could be set to trigger the explosion at any desired depth. The depth bomb had the typical bomb shape and the depth charge had a barrel shape. Depth charges were usually delivered by rolling them off a track located on the stern of the anti-submarine vessel, or they were hurled off the vessel's side in pairs by means of a "Y" shape device called a Y-gun. Neither weapon required contact with a submarine to destroy it. Since water is incompressible, any explosion beneath the surface causes the water to be forced away from it in all directions. The purpose of the depth bomb or depth charge was to rapidly increase the water pressure on a submarine's hull and rupture the hull near the area of explosion. As a submarine's depth increased, there was a corresponding increase in the normal water pressure, consequently, the more effective any explosion would be. Stressed to the limit, our boat's hull, which was less than an inch thick, could be considered flimsy.)

After considerable effort, the source of the air activity was pinpointed. We reported the information, and our reporting resulted in the eventual destruction of an important military airport by American bombs.

The waters at the southern end of Mindanao seemed promising, especially the Davao Gulf. As we were standing off the gulf's mouth, the skipper observed a properly-marked hospital ship entering the

3

mouth bound for Davao. No shooting there. The next day the same ship came out and made her way north.

Finally the skipper's diligence proved his thinking to be correct. We were able to get in position for a submerged attack on a small convoy, an attack which did not go as well as we had hoped, and for which we literally paid in sweat.

Rivulets of perspiration ran across the control room deck as the boat listed slightly. The temperature was 129° F. Atmospheric pressure in the boat was higher than normal, due to the presence of high pressure air used to initiate the ejection of torpedoes from their tubes. That air was bled back into the boat before the torpedoes completely left the tubes. A further increase in our atmospheric pressure was caused by the addition of oxygen from special containers, to replace that which our bodies consumed. An even greater factor in the temperature discomfort was the high relative humidity which prevented significant evaporation of perspiration.

As our bodies consumed oxygen, they gave off carbon dioxide, which could become toxic if it continued to increase. We spread a granular carbon dioxide-absorbing chemical on mattress covers placed on the deck in the forward torpedo room, in the dining room and in the after torpedo room.

Several hours ago we dived with four hot engines. All the heat from the engines was trapped within the hull of the *Flying Fish*. The warm waters of the Pacific were cool by comparison, but cork insulation lining the hull's interior prevented any appreciable heat transfer.

By chancing detection and running at high speed, we were able to get near an intercept course of a small convoy of ships. Our shooting position was not good, but our attack resulted in one hit which damaged a freighter. After that, we paid the price, dodging the enemy but not being able to completely escape. This was a typical seek and elude contest between destroyer and submarine.

There were two escort vessels with the convoy. The Japanese captains, apparently thinking there could be more than one American submarine in the area, were not taking any unnecessary chances. They made alternating runs on us, each taking turns at listening in the general area with their sonar and assisting each other in keeping us located. After a few runs, what we determined to be the smaller vessel broke off and returned to the convoy. The destroyer remained and continued the attack.

I was in the forward torpedo room, lying on my bunk, hanging onto the bunk's frame and watching the overhead. During one depth charge salvo, the hull overhead seemed to bulge downward at least one foot. I was surprised when it sprang back to its original position. For a brief moment the only sound I heard was the thumping of my heart as I brushed particles of insulation cork off my face. I wondered: "How far away were those depth charges, 35 feet away, 40 feet away? If the one which had caused the downward bulge in the hull had been one foot nearer, would the hull have held?"

The boat took a sharp angle. Now the explosions were near our stern. Our shipmates in the after torpedo room were getting the full effect of the explosions. The boat's angle increased alarmingly. The water pressure gauge translated into a bow depth of 327 feet. With our angle, that would put the stern near 400 feet. Our boat's recommended maximum depth was 300 feet.

A quiet voice said, "Damn, I wish this was one of the new boats. They can go to 600 feet or more."

Matt, in charge of the forward torpedo room and those crew members within it, displayed his annoyance with his typical finger-stabbing-the-air action; voicing it with, "Shut up! This old girl can take it. She's been through much worse than this."

Necessary corrections were made in the control room and we were soon back to our intended depth of 275 feet.

My thoughts reverted to my family back in Pennsylvania. "How long had it been since I had seen my parents, and will I ever see them again?" My mind raced on to Submarine School in New London, Connecticut, to the Submarine Base Relief crew at Brisbane, Australia, and to Alyce, the Australian girl I had been dating.

I told myself, "You asked for this. The Chief at the Brisbane dry dock tried to talk you out of your stupid kid desire to serve on a fighting submarine. You don't feel so damn important now, do you? And what about Alyce? You were just getting to know and appreciate her. Australia has some very nice people and Alyce has to be one of the nicest. You could be enjoying a picnic lunch with her at this very moment. But no, you were going to show those Japs. Then there was the boxing coach at the Submarine Base who tried to talk you into becoming a member of his team. You could be walking the streets of New London enjoying the sunshine." My thoughts were broken by the arrival of our engineering officer.

We had given our damage report to the conning tower by phone. That didn't satisfy our engineering officer, whom we called "Slue-foot." I don't know what Matt's true feelings were towards him, but as our unofficial nomenclator, it was he who dubbed him "Slue-foot." It was a name he rightly earned. He had very heavy feet. He made a quick, glancing inspection, turned and went plopping down the passageway towards the control room, but not before he cautioned us not to make any noise. Sound travels well through water, and a sharp sound, such as a wrench striking the metal deck could have put us in greater peril, if it was picked up on enemy sonar.

Matt grumbled, "Damn feather merchant." (This was a non-flattering name used by regular navy personnel to designate reserve officers.) "He sounds like a seal out of water going down that passageway. Skipper should make him go without shoes. We don't need him to tell us how to handle ourselves in this room during silent running. Shit, I've been through three times as many depth charge attacks as he's had years in this man's Navy. I've had more ash cans (depth charges) explode around me than he's had nights of shore leave. I'm in charge of this room and I'll tell you what to do, and when I say it, you'd better listen. Now I'm telling you not to make half the noise he made going down the passageway. Skipper ought to make him go barefoot."

I was called to the control room. Work relief lines had been formed to spell the planes-men. I was first in a line of three to relieve Schoonmaker, a gunner's mate trainee. Wet with sweat, he looked exhausted. With the hydraulic system shut down for silent running, all operation of the planes was manual, by brute force. The wheel of the helm and the planes wheels are similar, but the helmsman in the conning tower above us had a stool to sit on where he faced a compass and kept the course. Those on the planes did not have the luxury of a stool. Manning the planes required greater force and more frequent changing of the wheel's position than the demands of the helm. A standing position gave one greater leverage.

Planes-men stood facing a bubble, not unlike a carpenter's level bubble and worked to keep the boat at a desired depth. Depending upon the demands of physical exertion required and the man's endurance, each operator would fall back to the third position after about 10 minutes of exhausting work. The work was not as debilitating as the conditions — the foul air and the high temperature. R.D. Sproull, my forward room buddy who was on the stern planes, seemed to be less fatigued than Schoonmaker, who, on the bow planes, was struggling to hold a level bubble.

The skipper, standing near the diving officer, studying the navigation chart and occasionally observing the performance of men in the control room, spoke quietly but firmly, "Schoonmaker, dammit, keep that bubble level."

Schoonmaker did not accept the skipper's reprimand well. He turned his back to the planes control wheel, faced the skipper and said, "Don't you Goddamn me, Goddamn you!"

The skipper, Robert D. Risser, U.S. Navy Commander and captain of the *Flying Fish*, handled the possibly serious confrontation with the compassion of a father and judgment of a diplomat. In a soft voice he said, "Get back on the planes, Schoonmaker." Then he turned to the chart table beside him. Schoonmaker, Seaman First Class, stared at Commander's Risser's back for a moment, before returning to his assigned task.

Quietly propelling at a speed equal to a normal walk, the *Flying Fish* changed courses and performed many different maneuvering tactics in an effort to lose the enemy above. At times it appeared that the enemy was randomly searching. Then, the distant pinging sounds of the sonar searching would become distinct and soon would be striking our hull with sharp clarity. Another depth charge attack would follow. Their sound man was good.

We fired a noisemaker, a device resembling a tiny torpedo. Its sound and speed were intended to simulate those of a submarine. It confused their sound man and led them away for a short time but they were soon back in our general area. That sound man was VERY good.

With any kind of luck we would find a thermal barrier, an area of water where the temperature and salinity varied from that above. Such a condition caused sonar soundings to be deflected. No such luck.

The SWISH - SWISH - SWISH - SWISH sounds of the destroyer's propellers came again from directly above us. I thought, "He's near enough to hit with potatoes if I were on the surface." I wondered, "Can I throw a potato 275 feet?" I don't know why I thought about throwing potatoes. It must have been the farm boy in me. But I don't remember ever throwing potatoes at anything.

"Helluva situation to be in. Why doesn't the skipper wait until the ash cans explode, blow all ballast tanks, come bursting out of the water and poke three torpedoes at him?" Then I chastised myself for such reckless thinking. Such action could possibly succeed, but the odds highly favored the enemy in an outright challenge. Any destroyer, with its many and varied guns fully manned and at battle stations, would blow us out of the water before we could even get to our one major gun, a puny four-incher located on the afterdeck. Our surface fire power, other than the torpedoes, was intended to be used on unarmed, poorly armed, or badly damaged vessels. There was a time to fight and a time to run. This was not the time to fight.

The attacks became fewer and less effective. I was hoping, "The bastard must be running out of depth charges." Fewer depth charges were dropped with each attack. Something else was working to our advantage: perhaps we had found a thermal barrier. His last two deliveries were not very close. A last series of explosions which sounded several hundred feet away, and then there were no more. Our sound man lost their propeller noise. "Did the destroyer leave or were the Japanese just lying in wait until we did something foolish?" We continued our cautious silent running for another 15 minutes. Slowly and quietly we came to periscope depth. Nothing except ocean showing!

We secured from silent running and I returned to the forward torpedo room where I sat down on the nearest bunk. Bennett, making it known that he was speaking to the four newcomers, asked, "Well, how did you like your initiation?"

Evans probably spoke for all of us, including Bennett, when he responded, "I'd rather be in Brisbane."

The air in the boat was foul and the temperature was nearly unbearable. Everyone had a headache and fatigue had taken its toll. The ship's batteries, which had a great demand placed upon them during our attack approach, were now getting low. All of these things would be corrected. After some precautionary measures, we would surface, force cooling, refreshing air through the boat and put our batteries on charge. I don't know which I thought to be most important, but charged batteries meant survival under water. We bagged up the spent carbon dioxide absorbent, cleaned up some insulation bits and the glass from one gauge. Then we relaxed and waited for the Klaxon to herald our call to the surface.

The fresh air, like a breath of new life, bathed our faces. Each of us in the room took breath after deep breath, washing our lungs with the cool, fresh air which was flowing through the boat.

Thorough examination revealed no serious damage apparent anywhere outside or inside the hull of the *Flying Fish*. We made our way from the gulf area, and while recharging our batteries, headed toward the shipping lanes between the Davao Gulf and Palau. The Davao Gulf would be heavily patrolled for a while.

We hunted unsuccessfully in those shipping lanes for two days, during which time enemy plane activity occupied most of our attention. We were happy when we were ordered, via coded message, to the submarine tender *USS Orion* which was anchored in a northern New Guinea harbor.

We were tied up to the *Orion* for 48 hours. There was enough time to enjoy the amenities a large ship could offer. While we were resting, the *Orion's* relief crew worked on our ship.

Two engine exhaust valves damaged during the depth charge attack had to be replaced. The expended torpedoes were replaced, our food supply brought up to capacity, fresh water and fuel tanks were filled.

While the work was being done, our crew, in small groups and at spaced intervals, was transported to a remote, sandy beach by one of the *Orion's* launches. This was done in a rotation pattern, leaving a sufficient number of men on board to man the ship if necessary. We were provided with some baseball equipment and a very large supply of beer; then the launch returned to the *Orion*. The crew had been under great stress for more than two continuous weeks and I suppose this outing was intended to help wash our minds.

Matt was in charge of our group. We tossed baseballs around for awhile, but didn't work up a game. We swam in the warm water and enjoyed the fantastic sea-life. We were amazed at the variety of beautiful sea shells on the beach and by the living representatives in the water. We cornered a large octopus and tormented it for entertainment. Mostly, we drank beer, relaxed, soaked up the sun and talked.

The launch returned at a predetermined time. Much beer remained, all warm. Most of us were ready to return to the familiar comfort of the *Flying Fish*. The brief break was a nice change but it was not fulfilling. We returned with varied degrees of sunburn. Even the lookouts were somewhat deprived of sunlight while at sea. Those with duties within the hull got topside rarely, and then only by asking the bridge officer for permission. In an emergency dive situation, the officer on the deck did not want any delay before pulling the plug. Someone of higher rating from the engine room who hadn't stood lookout in a year or more could not remotely match the speed with which the regular lookouts exited the bridge. During an emergency dive, a second could mean the difference between life and death.

When we returned to our ship, I learned that a member of the after torpedo room had been transferred and replaced by John J. Peterman, Torpedoman Second Class. John had served on the *Flying Fish* throughout his sea duty experience. He was a member of her crew when she was commissioned in December of 1941, and was on her during the first six or seven war patrols she made, then he was assigned shore duty.

Somehow his name sounded familiar. I went aft to meet the torpedoman, who seemed to be held in high esteem by anyone who knew him. To my surprise, he was a person I had met, purely by chance, just after I graduated from basic training. We were both on leave and met in my hometown. Seeing his submarine insignia, I introduced myself and we visited. John was very modest, and I didn't learn that he was a veteran of several war patrols even then. He was not wearing his combat pin or any of the service ribbons he had been awarded. (The combat pin is a silver submarine with small gold stars attached for each successful war patrol.)

John, who was called "Pete" by most of the crew, came from a town some 40 miles from my hometown. Our casual meeting ended. I hadn't even learned the name of the submarine on which he served, this was not unusual, as very little was told during that time of war. This was especially true in the case of submariners. Pete and I quickly became closer friends and later became co-gunners on the ship's 40-millimeter gun.

Fully loaded and under escort, the *Flying Fish* headed in the direction of the enemy waters from which she had returned. Our new assignment was more in the order of a humane charge as compared to the previous one.

There were activities other than those of a brutal nature carried out by submarines, e.g. rescue mission of both civilians and fighting personnel. Also, information gathering, through periscope observation or by getting intelligence personnel into areas otherwise inaccessible.

A Celebes Island invasion was in the making. There would be much air activity to soften up the Japanese forces controlling the island. The *Flying Fish* and several other submarines strategically positioned throughout the area would cruise their assigned positions, remaining on the surface day and night prepared to pick up downed pilots.

After the Pearl Harbor bombing the Japanese began taking over islands between their homeland and the Hawaiian Islands, adding to those already part of their Empire. With the exception of Australia, they controlled the sea and land between Japan, the tiny island of Midway, and the Hawaiian Islands.

Their control of the seas included a vast area, extending northeast of Japan to the Aleutian Islands, southeast beyond the equator to the Gilbert Islands, southwest to the Netherlands East Indies and Sumatra, then on to the borders of China and Russia in an arc which included Thailand and Burma. They had free rein and were hindered only by our submarines until our other military forces got mobilized. With great cost in American lives, our forces were pushing the enemy back island by hard-fought island and nearing the Japanese mainland, which if necessary would be our final conquest of the war. The Celebes and Borneo were the two largest islands south of the Philippines still controlled by the Japanese. That too would change and our submarines would continue to play a role in that change.

Chapter 2

The Making of a Submariner

From high school in a small coal mining community where I and my family lived after selling our farm six years earlier, into the U.S. Navy and Submarine Service: It was no problem for the Navy and an adventure for me.

The year was 1943. War fever was at its peak. The sneak attack the Japanese had made on Pearl Harbor was still fresh in everyone's mind. Songwriters were playing on the Pearl Harbor attack and on other war events. Songs such as "Remember Pearl Harbor" stirred anger against our enemies while others like "Praise the Lord and Pass the Ammunition" highlighted the courageous sacrifices and exploits of our fighting men. The lyrics of the second song were —

> Praise the Lord and pass the ammunition.
> Praise the Lord and pass the ammunition.
> Praise the Lord and pass the ammunition,
> And we'll all stay free.
>
> The Sky-Pilot said it,
> You gotta give him credit
> For a son of a gun of a gunner was he.

Still others tugged at our heartstrings. One of the most popular was "Don't Sit Under the Apple Tree with Anyone Else but Me." (Many of you reading this are familiar with this song. Even today, it still enjoys a fair degree of popularity.)

As in any war, and as is typical of any nation's government during a time of war, ours had cranked up the propaganda machines, further promoting patriotism which was running at high pitch. The efforts of our country and those of our people were focused upon war-related activities.

Industry capitalized on the war theme. Some clothing for children was designed after military uniforms, and the caramel coated popcorn, Cracker Jack, was boxed with war toys and cards depicting enemy aircraft to encourage children and adults to be on the lookout for such aircraft.

Gasoline was rationed and automobile tires could be obtained only by special permit. The automobile speed limit was 35 mph to conserve gasoline. Meat and sugar were two of several foods rationed. There were few complaints from the civilian population about those or any of the other inconveniences. Housewives saved cooking fats which could be used in the manufacture of explosives. Tin cans were saved, mainly to salvage the small amount of tin which coated those cans. Our nation and our people were involved in an all-out war effort.

In my community of less than 1,000 residents, most homes displayed a banner representing family members serving in our armed forces. Our home displayed two such banners. We also displayed one representing an awarded Purple Heart. I had one brother on the European Front and one in the South Pacific. The brother serving on the European Front, where he had been wounded, recovered from his wound and was back in the thick of things again. Our little community had suffered from the war. A neighbor two houses east of us died on Guadalcanal, in the South Pacific. A neighbor who lived next door and west of us was killed on the European Front. Several other men from our tiny community had been killed in action, one during the Pearl Harbor attack. In our small community, these were young men known by all. Their death was considered a personal loss, felt almost as strongly as if they were family members. War was a reality. Ours was a determined and angry community. Ours was a determined and angry nation. The American people were caught up in the emotionalism of war and I was no exception. Nor was I an exception to the generalization that blood runs hot in the young. I had just graduated from high school and considered myself very much a man. I was anxious to share the excitement, the adventure, the "glory" of combat. I had no true concept of the facts of war. I was a boy. My patriotism had reached a frenzied state and each reported "missing in action," "killed or wounded in action," kept it at that level.

Within days of my graduation from high school, I was drafted into the armed forces. I had a choice of Army or Navy. I chose the Navy. My only experience with boats was one short ferryboat ride and two or three fishing trips in a rowboat. Most of my experiences with bodies of water came from sitting on the bank of a pond or stream while I fished. I could swim but could not be considered a good swimmer. None of my previous life activities seemed even remotely related to the Navy and even less to Submarine Service. Nevertheless, I was to become a submariner.

As a kid, I was fascinated with the phenomenon

of sound traveling through water. In our swimming hole, my siblings and I tapped out coded messages under water with rocks while we listened beneath the water's surface. We experimented with different distances and different degrees of water turbulence. I'm not at all sure that this in any way helped me to become a better submariner. It did give me some standard for measuring the distance of the enemy's propellers and the distance of the depth charges which were dropped near the hull of the *Flying Fish*. Perhaps total ignorance would have been more desirable. I would not have been as able to visualize the danger outside our hull as well.

The Navy, in its wisdom, appeared unconcerned with detailed background information on any individual. All of those elements that made up what I was didn't seem to matter. The Navy had its own standards and methods. In my case they seemed to work.

I was selected as a future submariner after just six weeks, near the end of my basic training period. Basic Training Camp (Boot Camp), was not a pleasant experience for most trainees. Exercises were rigorous and rules were strict. Some trainees complained about the food, about the strenuous workouts, the dictatorial treatment, the tight schedule and the lack of time to properly shave and dress before being marched off to breakfast. To me, none of those things were a problem. The food was good and there was a lot of it. As a teenager, I was not a finicky eater. I welcomed the physical demands of the training program. I had been boxing as an amateur and had disciplined my mind and body to a regular training program of demanding exercise. My body was in excellent condition. I found the group exercises more enjoyable than when I worked out alone or with our small group of boxers. The tight morning schedule didn't bother me. I didn't concern myself much about shaving, so that gave me extra time in the morning.

About the second week, during inspection, our Company Chief asked me when I had last shaved. When I answered, "A few days ago," he replied, "Hereafter, shave that peach-fuzz off your face every day." His command, though forceful, did not have the tone of a reprimand. There must have been many others in our company who had nothing but peach-fuzz on their faces. Looking back on that incident today, the chief must have thought, "My God! We're sending babies to war." I fulfilled that seemingly unnecessary task each day. But I did it before turning in at night, leaving my mornings less hectic than that of others.

I was one of several in camp who suffered from an affliction called Sampsonitus. Sampsonitus, named after Camp Sampson was nothing to fool with. Once having suffered this condition, the trainee never experienced it again. A sort of trained immunity was imprinted on the mind and on the affected body parts. The condition developed when a trainee sat on the edge of his bunk in the nude. Under the right conditions, the bunk springs would be pressed down and away from the bunk frame. This allowed the testicles of an unsuspecting trainee to drop between the spring and the frame. A sudden forward motion would result in a painful and often bruising extrication of the testicles, which became trapped when the spring returned to its normal position. To compound things, I was on the top bunk and had jumped off.

With much pain and even more concern, I reported to sick bay. After a quick examination the doctor told me that I would soon be back to normal. He said, with a teasing smile on his face, "Don't worry, you'll be able to carry out any manly duties expected of you. That is, if you ever get the chance." I walked out of his office thinking, "Wise guy. It wouldn't be so funny if he had the problem." Since this occurred early in the morning, I was given the entire day to rest. The next morning, still hurting and very sore, I was returned to the ranks.

There were 200 trainees in our company. From this 200, I was one of three who were selected as being qualified   for   either   submarine   duty   or   deep-sea diving. I don't know what criteria was used in the selection. I suppose the intelligence, psychological, and physical tests were used as standards. These branches of the service were strictly voluntary. After much thought, I accepted the opportunity to serve on a submarine.

My choice made, the Navy decided that I should become a torpedoman and I was shipped off to torpedo school in Norfolk, Virginia. Sometime during my training period at Norfolk, I was given another physical examination. A disappointing outcome! My front teeth did not meet well enough to properly hold the mouth piece on the submarine escape apparatus. I thought that evaluation to be rather stupid. In my thinking, if a submarine was sunk, either all on board would be dead or the depth would be too great for the apparatus to be useful. The apparatus had limited capability with a 150-foot depth maximum. Nonetheless, I was deemed unfit for submarine duty. I was to continue in torpedo school in preparation for serving on a surface vessel. At this point I was wishing I had chosen duty as a deep-sea diver. But then, my teeth might have been a problem there also.

The torpedo school was just that, a torpedo school. There was no distinction between torpedoes used by submarines and those used by destroyers, P.T. boats, destroyer escorts, or any other vessel which carried torpedoes.

During the early stages of the course, all of our studies, and all of the instruction was much like most classroom courses, strictly textbook and lecture. As we advanced in our studies, we often went to the repair shop where we would disassemble and later reassemble torpedoes.

When graduation came, those qualified to be submariners were processed for transfer to submarine school. The torpedo school had one small problem, it was several men short of the quota. A request was made for volunteers. We were told that it was merely to fill the quota, that once we reached the submarine base we would be given another physical examination and after we failed the examination we would be transferred to destroyer duty. What was to be lost? I volunteered.

The second day at the New London, Connecticut, Submarine Base was test time. I was annoyed, angered, and embarrassed by some of the probing and personal questions asked during the oral psychological test. When I responded to such questions, my voice gave evidence of my anger. In my untrained mind, I could see no connection between the probing questions and submarine duty. Then came the physical examination. The examination was thorough and complete up to a point. The doctor never looked into my mouth. Our Navy must have needed submariners badly.

Submarine school went well. In theory, every man on board a submarine was expected to be able to assume, with some degree of efficiency, any task on the ship. An impossible expectation, but we did learn, in a general way, the functions of the entire ship.

The dreaded day for practicing deep water escape came. First, with an instructor, we were placed in a pressure chamber where we were subjected to air pressure greater than that which we would experience within the escape chamber. Our fleet submarines had an escape hatch attached to and above the forward torpedo room.

After clearing that obstacle, we were introduced to the escape apparatus, called a Momsen lung. This device, a charged air-bag with a carbon dioxide absorbent in it, would accept an air pressure charge equal to the external pressure and would slowly reduce its internal pressure as the outside pressure was reduced. Chambers identical to those on submarines, were attached to a 100-foot water tower at the 25-, 50- and 100-foot levels. Each trainee entered the chamber from the outside with an instructor. The entry hatch was secured just as the entry hatch on a submarine would be secured, separating the escapee or escapees from a flooding submarine. There was a second hatch between the chamber and the water in the tower which represented the sea. That hatch, the escape hatch, was closed, dogged down and held tightly shut by the external water pressure. This escape hatch, came up shoulder height to the seated men, making it possible to trap the air above the shoulders in the chamber when this exit hatch was opened. The air below the shoulders would be replaced by the entering water, but the air pressure above, which was equal to the water pressure, would keep the chamber's upper portion free from water.

Within the chamber, after the instructor had gone over the procedure in a step-by-step dry run, a valve was opened allowing water from the tower to fill the chamber to the top of the escape hatch. Then a high pressure air valve was opened and pressure was slowly allowed to build up until it equaled the external water pressure showing on a gauge. When the air pressure neared that of the water, the escape hatch was undogged permitting it to be opened when the two pressures were equal. The air-bag was charged with air, a buoy attached to a line released, and with the Momsen lung's mouthpiece firmly gripped between the teeth, the escapee exited the escape chamber. Using the buoy line as a guide and as a means of preventing rapid surfacing, he slowly moved up the line, while breathing normally. This allowed the pressure in the body to adjust to that of the lessening water pressure as the air in the air-bag escaped and matched the external pressure.

The first surfacing was from 25 feet as a confidence builder. Then a surfacing was made from a depth of 50 feet. At both the 25-foot and 50-foot depths, the instructor followed the trainee out through the hatch without benefit of the Momsen lung, and swimming freely, stayed with the trainee for the first 50 or 60 seconds. At the 100-foot level, an instructor came out of the 50-foot level chamber to meet us. I'm sure the instructor was there as a precautionary measure as well as for instruction in the event that our form was incorrect, but to me, his being there was an additional confidence builder. He was there without aid of the escape apparatus.

At the 50- and 100-foot levels, I held the mouthpiece as much with my lips as I did with my teeth, but I did hold it. I was not concerned about ever using the apparatus again. Rightly or wrongly, I felt that the need for ever using the escape apparatus was too small to even consider. My mind was firmly set on being a submariner.

There were 10 or 12 trainees at that training session. Of these, one came up from the 50-foot depth with some blood coming from one ear. That ended his submarine potential and perhaps his military service.

With doubts of the escape apparatus behind me, I was ready to assume my responsibilities. With school nearing completion, we began putting into practice some of the teaching by making periodic visits to a training submarine which was tied up at a nearby dock. From that stage, we advanced to the actual thing, where we took the boat down the Thames River and out to sea.

I had expected us to be grouped into our specific areas of expected expertise. This was very naive thinking on my part. At this early stage in our degree of advancement, our duties would be general and less sophisticated in nature. Specific training in our intended areas of specialty would come when we were serving on our assigned submarines. Under close supervision, we were given various tasks to perform. We were instructed, corrected and reinstructed. We were being trained to serve on a fighting submarine, and as we were reminded again and again — "This duty leaves little or no margin for error!"

One of the most enjoyable classroom sessions was held in the torpedo simulation-firing room. This room had a very large table in the center, not unlike a billiard table, except that it was many times larger. The table had miniature ships on it and they moved, on small tracks, over its surface. We were given the opportunity to plot the course and speed, and to fire torpedoes to intercept the vessels. The "torpedoes," when fired by means of an electric switch, advanced as torpedo-shaped lights from bulb to bulb until they passed under the intended target, or passed by as a miss.

Although this type of training was a regular part of the officers' training program and had no part in any specific task we would be called upon to perform, it did serve to give us a more complete picture of a torpedo attack. By today's standards this was a very simple and crude but effective device.

I enjoyed the school and learned my lessons well. The written examinations were routine, my grades were excellent and I was proud of my accomplishments. With the realization that my true tests and learning still lay ahead of me, I was eager to get on with it, get into the fight and help win the war. I was a typical young wartime American.

Throughout our submarine school training period we did daily marching and calisthenics. These were minimal and did not satisfy my acquired exercise regime. I went to the base gymnasium to see what kind of facilities they had. I didn't get much time to look around before the boxing coach began to question me. He moved quickly in his desire to evaluate my potential and I, suited up in proper attire he provided, found myself in the ring. My opponent, though of questionable ability, was heavier than I and must have made me look good. The coach, in his effort to recruit me as a team member, asked me to return the next day. Then he made the mistake of telling me what a great opportunity it would be if I was good enough to make the team. I would stay on the Base as a permanent member of the club, I would get lots of liberties and frequent leaves. The rosy picture he painted didn't require any momentous decision on my part. Being an innocent, hot-blooded boy, pumped full of patriotism, I wanted to serve on a fighting submarine. I wanted to get my licks in. "We'd show those Japs!"

During the remaining weeks at the base, I visited the gymnasium several times. Once, I even went back into the ring with one of the better boxers. Again the coach asked if I was interested in becoming a member of the team. After receiving my negative answer, he tended to ignore me whenever I showed up thereafter.

Even after the submarine school graduation ceremony was held, I still had concerns about a final physical examination which would preclude my total acceptance as a submariner, but I had no reason for concern.

Soon I was on a slow troop train heading for an embarkation point in the San Francisco area. Final destination: the submarine tender *USS Sperry*, located in Milne Bay, New Guinea. There I would await further orders.

Chapter 3

Shipping Out

Quartered in what previously were first-class accommodations on a former luxury liner, we submariners had a feeling of special importance. We were granted privileges far beyond that which any lowly young sailor could expect. The *USS America*, now a troop transport, was packed with sailors, soldiers, and marines whose quarters were anything but pleasant, unless they were officers, or, as in our case, submarine sailors. With few exceptions, we were all recent graduates of the Submarine School and there wasn't an officer among us. Perhaps we were given those quarters because there were fewer than 100 of us, but we all felt that we were given preferential treatment because we were submariners. This thought made us feel proud and important.

Billeted in cabins for two on the main deck, with private showers, how could anyone feel anything but flattered? My cabin mate was Raymond D. Sproull. R.D. and I went through submarine school together, but we did not know each other until we became cabin mates. R.D. was good company. This was the way to live. Our luxury became much more evident after walking through much of the ship. On the lower decks, the men were crowded into large open areas, bunks tightly fitted together allowing limited space for narrow passageways. Toilet facilities were limited and there were no showers available. On the third deck below our quarters, a stopped-up toilet or toilets had overflowed, and the deck of the toilet room was a filthy mess.

Yes, being a submarine sailor had its benefits. We walked the main deck, enjoyed the warm sun, chatted with the nurses who were billeted in cabins adjacent to ours, and in general, adapted happily to our temporary position of aristocracy.

After being escorted out to sea, the *America* traveled without escort. We were safer without it. Very few escort vessels could equal her speed, and it would be a near miracle for any enemy submarine to be in position to intercept us in our zigzag pattern with our superior speed. Danger from enemy planes was even more remote. The relatively short-ranged planes needed a base and that would mean an aircraft carrier. Our submarines, surface ships, and planes were constantly searching for such targets. At this point in the war, the Japanese surface ships had been pushed into their own waters, beyond our destination.

The passage ended too quickly and we were in Milne Bay, New Guinea. There, we temporarily got lost in the shuffle and along with several other sailors we submariners were transported to a shore station. Our temporary home was a barracks not far from the mess hall. This was more than acceptable to me. We had no duties assigned to us other than to be present for morning roll call.

On the second morning, a fellow sailor and I walked down a dusty road which had been newly plowed through the dense jungle. We met three sailors who were from the 104th Naval Construction

Battalion. This was a near unbelievable and joyous surprise. My brother Martin was assigned to that group. A short walk took us directly to his tent. An occupant of a near-by tent told us that he had gone to get a look at the former luxury liner which was anchored in the bay. We waited. His surprise was exceeded by his pleasure. His surprise to see me was even greater than mine to find him there. I knew he was somewhere in the Pacific area. He thought I was still in the States.

That day and the next, we visited. We wrote a joint letter to our family and continued to marvel at the fortunate chance meeting. We had not seen each other for nearly a year and had a lot of catching up to do. Our conversations covered a wide range of topics, light and serious. One of our greatest concerns was for our brother Michael, who had been wounded on the European front, had recovered from the wound, and was back in another European battle area.

Then I was transferred to the submarine tender, *USS Sperry* which was anchored in the bay. A submarine tender was a medium-sized ship designed to act as a mother-ship for submarines. Her crew was made up of knowledgeable submariners and other specialists capable of making any revisions or repairs which did not require dry dock facilities. Tenders carried most spare parts a submarine could need, as well as torpedoes, ammunition, fuel and food.

It was several days before I could get back to my brother's base, only to find that the 104th had shipped out. This left me with concern for his safety and with my first twinge of homesickness. We did not see each other again until the war ended. To this day, we marvel at that chance meeting and the smallness of the world.

While assigned to the *Sperry*, I helped scrape and paint the conning tower of a submarine which was preparing for a war patrol. That job lasted one day, and I was assigned as the third member, in lowest position, on a three-man ship-to-shore launch. This assignment lasted about three weeks. We lived in a large tent on shore with several other men, and our duty was to transfer supplies to and from the ship, a pleasant and relaxed three weeks during which few demands were made for our services. Most of the time, we were left to while away the days.

The two petty officers with whom I shared the launch treated me as an equal and were helpful in instructing me about the operations and handling of the craft. They were also navy-wise and knew all the angles. One moonlit night we took the launch out to a cove hidden from the base and the tender and did some water skiing. We skied on a makeshift planing board. The board was rounded in front with two rope handles attached and the tow rope fastened to the board, between the handles. When the launch was brought up to speed, the board planed nicely.

Even I, unexperienced as I was, realized that our action would draw serious punishment if it became known, especially since we were adding to our breach of regulations by drinking alcoholic beverages. This was my first introduction to torpedo juice, a mixture of grain alcohol and orange juice. The pure grain alcohol, a combustion fuel required for torpedoes, was a potent form of vodka; vodka, without the added water content. Usually it was denatured through the addition of a substance which rendered it unpalatable and dangerous if consumed. Most savvy navy men knew how to get the pure stuff from the supply depot. My two shipmates were savvy.

That experience ended all too quickly and I was given, with about 20 other sailors, which included R.D. Sproull, passage to Australia on a sea-going tugboat. We took turns in standing lookout watch during the three or four-day trip. My assigned station was the crow's nest high above the deck and as the tug listed I could look down and see nothing but water beneath me, this gave me my first suggestion of seasickness. I wasn't concerned, I thought it was a thing sea-time would correct. It didn't. I remained seasick prone.

Arriving in Brisbane without any fanfare, we were assigned to the Submarine Base Relief Crew and given quarters in a nearby barracks. The relief crew work in Brisbane was much more sophisticated than that on any tender. The work was done in dry dock and few major repairs were beyond the capability of the experienced crew.

Life became a routine of morning roll call, three square meals and since I had no area of true expertise, the most menial tasks on the relief crew: the tasks of cleaning up, scraping the hull, chipping rust and painting. It was much like an eight-to-five civilian job except for those weeks when I was assigned to additional guard duty or was required to stand additional fire watch on a special welding project. There were no morning calisthenics. We simply assembled on the dock for roll call and then were assigned to specific work crews or duties. I enjoyed life. There was much to see and much to do, all of which was exciting and new to me. Most weeks I had two free days and liberty in Brisbane if I so chose.

I met Alyce, an Australian girl, at a Brisbane ballroom where we danced the jitterbug most of the night. We met again the next night and the affair began. We dated regularly. Alyce was a petite brunette who worked in a local woolen mill. She was a quiet, attractive girl and our relationship, though not a wild and exciting love affair, was a happy one. The thought that I should be doing more for the war effort kept nagging me. I was trained to be a submariner, a sea-going submariner. How would I feel going back home after the war without having directly fought the enemy? My teenage recklessness demanded that I get into the fight and help win the war. I made a request to be assigned to a submarine rather than wait until they got around to me.

All relief crews served as a replacement pool for transferees from submarines. Relief crews were a rich supply source made up of personnel with varied degrees of experience and expertise, ranging from those with very little to proven war-seasoned veterans.

When I told Alyce, she accepted my decision stoically. Before America had gained control of the waters around Australia, the Australian people expected to be invaded by the Japanese. All able-bodied men were serving in the armed forces, many of them on some remote island in the Pacific. Her family had not heard from her brother in months, and they assumed he was on one of those islands. She knew of the decisions and concerns war brought.

Our relationship was intimate but we made no verbal commitment. As if by tacit agreement, the relationship was a temporary one. Perhaps we were not totally compatible. During our five weeks of dating, she never took me to her home to meet her family and I had no desire to do so. I did not want to complicate my life. I had a caring family of parents and siblings halfway across the world and the bulk of my love was focused on them. Besides, I had a war to fight and any future commitment would have to wait.

Chapter 4

Welcome Aboard

The event: a beer bash in a primitive park several miles away from the city of Brisbane, Australia. Three days ago I was a member of the Submarine Base Relief Crew and now I was a member of the *Flying Fish* crew.

The new assignment came quickly. It had been little more than a week since I asked to be placed on a submarine. The *Flying Fish* was the first boat to arrive since I made my request to the chief in charge of the relief crew. The chief, a wise old veteran of submarine warfare, nodded his head with a look of understanding; then, as if compelled to make an effort to discourage the young man before him from his reckless desires, said, "Brisbane's a good liberty port. You should be happy here. Serving on a fighting submarine isn't any fun. Are you sure that this is what you really want?" I answered in the affirmative. He said, "All right, sooner or later you will be placed on one anyway." Before long, I would be indoctrinated into the real world of war.

Submarine skippers, as a usual procedure, made some changes in their crew after each patrol run. The reasons varied: The transfer of an individual who was deemed unsuited for submarine duty, duplication of ratings and responsibilities as a result of promotions, a request made by an individual for personal reasons, a man suffering from battle fatigue, and the perpetual need for additional submariners. Every submarine had a continuous training program in progress. This was battle training, training which carried the knowledge acquired in submarine school to a higher level of efficiency and coordination. Under those circumstances, and with responsibilities not highly critical, one learned during the actual fighting.

In the case of those who were deemed unsuitable for submarine warfare, the reasons also varied. They may not have met the qualification requirements in the allotted time. They may not have had personalities suitable for living in the confined submarine environment. Or, they may have shown signs of being unable to operate well under stress of battle or during depth charge attack.

Some of the transferees would go to newly constructed boats. Some would be assigned to positions as instructors at a school needing their expertise. Others would work in a relief crew or go to a base shop where their experience could contribute.

During her 10th war patrol, the *Flying Fish* had represented the submarine service and America well. She and her crew sank one medium-size freighter and severely damaged another of comparable size. They paid the price of a depth charge attack after each of their torpedo attacks. Now, with some minor damage from the depth charges, and other damage from the ravages of sea water, she was in dry dock getting repaired, and her crew was blowing off steam at the beer bash.

For me, the party was an experience of some educational value. Officers and crew members did not freely mingle. We were two groups, separated by a distance of several tables. It was obvious that the need for rank and authority which maintains the cohesiveness of any military entity could not be jeopardized even during a time of partying, especially during a time when nerves were still raw and the beer was flowing freely, with each group drinking its share. Later, at other parties and while at sea, I learned that the barrier between officers and enlisted men was not all that rigid.

This was my first meeting with the entire *Flying Fish* crew. There were no formal introductions, but before long I would get to know each of them well. The inner hull of a submarine is a very small place.

On the previous day, those of us new to the boat, and there were several of us, met with the Captain, Robert D. Risser, and the executive officer, Lieutenant Commander Julian T. Burke. There were no pep talks or instructions given during the meeting. It was simply an introductory meeting, and perhaps a chance for those key officers to take some measure of the new men upon whom they would need to depend. Later, we were turned over to the Chiefs or other designated heads of our respective specialties. These were the people who would act as our qualifying officers, the people under whose direct supervision and command we would be while on a work crew, and at times during battle.

John W. Mattingly, Torpedoman First Class, was the man in charge of the forward torpedo room. Matt, as he was known to all, was a career sailor. He joined the Navy when he was fresh out of high school, and even before Pearl Harbor was attacked he was a qualified submariner. Now at the age of 26, he was a well-seasoned warrior. He had served on some of our more primitive submarines before being assigned to the *Flying Fish*. Those submarines had a maximum safety depth capability of 200 feet. The *Flying Fish* had an additional 100 feet as an presumed safety margin. Matt knew what it was to sink ships and what it was to take a depth charge pounding. He respected the enemy, trusted his ship and his own skill, but doubted the ability of any new trainee until that individual began to show unquestionable progress.

Generally speaking, Matt was a mild mannered-man of average stature. When it came to his torpedo room, and his duty as the non-commissioned officer who recommended anyone serving under him in the room to be elevated to qualified submariner status, he was serious-minded and exacting. As he put it, "Before I give my okay for you to wear those qualifying dolphins on your sleeve, you'll need to know this boat in detail, from bow to stern. You'll be able to do everything from pumping the bilges to starting the engines." Stabbing an index finger in our direction, "On a submarine, you never know what an emergency situation will demand. When we're out there in the Japs' front yard, we go it alone. If we're in a tight spot, we expect no help and we get no help. Before long you'd better be able to do whatever the situation demands, without direction, and you damn well better do it well! Right now, you don't even know how to blow the head without it blowing back in your face."

Toilet waste was disposed of by sealing off the bowl by means of a valve controlled by foot pressure and with low pressure air, forcing the waste into the sanitary storage tank. The procedure required opening and closing a series of valves in proper sequence. Any deviation from that procedure could result in a very embarrassing accident. The submarine, a finely tuned and complicated vessel, didn't make allowance for any mistakes.

Again stabbing his finger through the air, "You'll learn everything and you'll learn it damn well. You screw up, not only in this torpedo room, but any place on the boat and get us killed, I'll chase your ass around Hell until you put the fire out!"

Standing nearby and smoking a cigarette, Wilfred A. Bennett, Torpedoman Third Class, grinned as he looked us over. Bennett, a qualified submariner, had probably heard something similar when he first became a crew member. He was a soft-spoken, rugged man, a little above average in height. He was usually quiet and always solidly dependable. He spoke to ask the question, "Do any of you know how to play cribbage?"

Matt asked, "What's that got to do with running a submarine?" Bennett, still grinning, and looking directly at Matt said, "Nothing, but I was hoping someone in the forward torpedo room could give me a little competition." Matt ignored the barb.

Matt had been in the Navy nine years. The Navy was his master, the *Flying Fish*, his mistress, and the forward torpedo room, his domain.

Castle J. Evans, Torpedoman Third Class; Raymond D. Sproull, Seaman First Class, and I, also a Seaman First Class, were replacements for three men transferred from the forward torpedo room of the *Flying Fish*. I did not know Evans until our first meeting on the boat. R.D. and I considered ourselves to be lucky. We not only got the same boat, but the bonus of the same torpedo room.

One other member, new to the forward torpedo room, was Robert Harding. Harding, Seaman First Class, though not a torpedoman trainee, would be one of the torpedo reload crew members. He was lucky, he got the spare bunk in the room. With the exception of the torpedo room gang, many of the crew members, through necessity, "hot bunked." When at sea with a full crew, bunk space was limited in the crews' sleeping area, so when a man went on duty, another coming off duty would often use the still-warm bunk. My duties changed slightly. I was still living on base and still working on a submarine which looked as if she had been dragged off the bottom after resting there for several years. I was still painting, after first chipping rust and the old paint. But there were greater and more important demands. Those of us who were being introduced to submarine duty for the first time had special and serious responsibilities. Evans, Sproull, and I would be required to qualify as submariners, and would be led through this challenging task by Matt. Harding would answer to a different qualifying officer. Evans, who was 16 months older than Sproull and I, had previously served on a cruiser before going to submarine school. He had been on Brisbane relief crew duty for more than three months. Like us, he was new to submarine sea-duty.

First, to be qualified as submariners and granted the privilege to wear the twin dolphin insignia, one had to show proof of knowing the boat's structure, important units within the boat, and the function of these units. This was done with required drawings representing compartments and all of the systems throughout the entire submarine. In addition, each new crew member had to prepare for an oral examination administered by the qualifying officer. The examination would be given when both parties agreed to a specific date and would involve a thorough bow-to-stern walk-through, with a question-and-answer session. There was no exception to this requirement, all officers and enlisted men went through it, and met the demands within a reasonable time frame. If they did not, they were assigned to surface vessels or became full-time relief crew members.

We quickly learned that Matt was very serious about his responsibility as a qualifying officer, and his brief talk to us at our first meeting took on greater meaning. In most cases the qualifying didn't begin until the boat was ready for sea. Matt had a different philosophy and acted on it. Even as Evans, Sproull and I were chipping rust off the ship's anchor, which was laid out on the dock, Matt stopped by to quiz us on some general point concerning the ship's operation. His first few quiz sessions always ended with, "Shit, you're not learning a damn thing." As time went on, the sessions began to end with a grunt, and still later, with nods of approval.

During one of those quiz-and-discussion periods, Matt's approach gave evidence of the wisdom of a man far older than his 26 years, "Learn the old girl inside and outside, learn about everything that makes her tick so that you can treat her well. She'll keep us alive only if she's able to do so; it's up to all of us to keep her that way." Then for no apparent reason, he turned to Harding, who was near by and said, "You're Stretch, Aren't you?"

Harding replied, "No, I'm Harding."

Matt, "No, you're Stretch all right."

As he walked away, Evans, Harding, and I looked at each other as we shook our heads in wonder. Evans said, "I guess you're Stretch." Matt's logic escaped us since Harding was only slightly above average in height. From that day on, he was "Stretch."

Sproull — R.D. to me — was several feet away

from us. If anyone within our immediate group fit the name "Stretch," it was he. At least four inches taller than Harding, he was one of the tallest men on the boat.

Matt looked back at R.D., "Pappy, you come with me. I've got another job for you."

R.D. asked, "You talking to me, Matt?"

"Yes, Pappy, come with me."

"Hey, Matt," R.D. objected, "I'm Sproull."

"No, you're Pappy. Now hop to it."

Matt and R.D. walked down the dock, leaving us bewildered and shaking our heads.

Later that day, I asked Matt why he tagged R.D. "Pappy." His answer was simply, "Because he's Pappy. Can't you see that?" When pressed further, his response was even more puzzling. "Because he looks like Pappy." When I asked who Pappy was, he answered, "Sproull."

That was the final word. It was obvious that the name "Pappy" was not intended in any derogatory sense. If anything, it seemed to have some sentimental attachment to it. Whatever the case, it wasn't long before all of us, including R.D., accepted his new name.

During my short period on this relief crew, I had worked on a submarine which had received considerable damage from depth charges. There was very little damage visible from the outside, but inside her after engine room, the overhead was nearly touching an engine where the hull bulged downward. The more knowledgeable submariners made comments about the miracle which kept the hull from bursting. Only now as a member of the *Flying Fish* crew, did the reality of my place in this war fully impress me. Knowingly, I and 87 or 88 other young men, led by

40

Commander Risser, who must have been all of 37 and the oldest man on the *Flying Fish*, would go into enemy waters in a solitary stalker with the intentions of attacking any worthwhile target. Only the high command and those of us on the submarine would know exactly what area of enemy water we were in. Whatever developed, there would be no one to come to our aid.

The greatest danger would be in attacking an enemy Naval Task Force, with its many destroyers and other anti-submarine ships. And yet, this was the ultimate quest of all submarine captains and crews. The ships of greatest value to the Japanese Navy would be there: the aircraft carriers, battleships, and cruisers. The time had come to face up to wartime facts. I was trained to serve on a submarine, but I was not a warrior. I was a year older and a bit wiser than when I had left basic training camp. I now needed a daily shave, but I was still a boy. The thought of sinking enemy ships was no longer a thing I was looking forward to. The sinking of ships meant the killing of other humans, something to which I had not given much thought before. And how well would I hold up under a depth charge attack?

The seriousness with which Matt approached his responsibility as a qualifying officer gave me a new outlook on submarine warfare. The environment in which the *Flying Fish* would be operating would be one of constant threat. Very little allowance existed for error. When submerged, a relatively fragile hull would be constantly under water pressure capable of flooding the entire vessel through even a small rupture. The deeper the *Flying Fish* submerged, the greater that pressure and the danger associated with it would be. We had to recognize and respect two enemies: the Japanese and the water pressure. This same hull, under the pressure of the water, would also be subjected to the extra explosive pressure of depth charges. Matt and the other experienced submariners accepted that as a fact, learned to live with it, and did everything they could to keep the vessel ready and at her best.

Several weeks went by. The *Flying Fish* was floated, removed from dry dock and ready to accept her crew. Even the mattress covers on the bunks had been changed. Throughout, she appeared to be spotless. The cleaning job was thorough. Now the time came for the crew to double check all functions of the ship before taking her out into deep water for several trial runs. We left the base barracks and moved into our quarters on the *Flying Fish*.

In the torpedo room, I had a comfortable bunk with a locker next to it just inches above a torpedo. I felt pretty much at home soon after coming on board. I had no thoughts of claustrophobia; the close quarters of the Flying Fish suited me just fine. The exterior length of my new home was 312 feet, and at the widest area it was 27 feet. The outer structures and the torpedo tubes in the torpedo rooms, gave the boat a deceiving appearance. The actual, interior length was about 220 feet, crammed with operating equipment, which with the exception of the dining area, control room, and the torpedo rooms, left only passageways. In my thinking, the forward torpedo room, although not spacious, was more than adequate.

The *Flying Fish* had accepted me, and I in turn adopted her. I had never known another ship and the dazzling array of valves, indicator lights and gauges were something submarine school had prepared me for. This was what I had volunteered for.

During the trial runs, Evans, Stretch, Harding, and I stood watches on the bow and stern planes (diving planes), the helm, and at lookout. During our free time, we worked on the qualifying demands. Everyone on the ship was willing to help and answered all questions in a simple and straightforward manner. They had all, from the skipper on down, been through the same thing and knew the importance of a well-trained crew in times of emergency. Matt continued to observe us in our efforts, but did so from a distance. He no longer quizzed us or urged us on. It was up to us to prove that we had the right stuff to become full-fledged submariners.

Trial runs were soon over. The ship, with the exception of a few minor adjustments, was ready for sea duty. Now it was time to fulfill the real purpose of a submarine during time of war.

With the exception of the torpedoes, all the supplies, food, ammunition and other items were brought on board by crew members. The torpedoes were placed on the respective decks, forward and aft, by special cranes, and as they reached the deck we, lowered them into the rooms through their loading hatches. The handling of the torpedoes was very demanding physical work. All of it was done with a chain-fall (a pulley system using chains rather than rope).

I had one last shore leave in Brisbane. Alyce and I assured each other that the *Flying Fish* would return to Brisbane after the war patrol. We both thought that Brisbane would become the boat's home port. Our parting was restrained, without any outward show of emotion. Similar to many wartime relationships, ours ended with a final kiss in the trolley, at the end of the track, near the Submarine Base entrance.

On August 1, 1944, less than 24 hours after we

started taking on supplies, we were being escorted out to open sea by an Australian destroyer escort, in the company of the *USS Flounder*, whose patrol area would be near ours. I thought the escort was there to protect us from any Japanese submarine which might be lurking outside the harbor. When I mentioned this during general conversation, Bennett laughingly said, "Hell, that's only about 30 percent of it. That escort's there to protect us from our own people and from the Aussies. Any submarine out there alone has 'Jap' written all over it in the eyes of those eager pilots. The destroyers and other surface ships aren't much better. The bastards all want to be heroes so bad they wouldn't even consider the possibility that we're American."

As we proceeded towards our designated station in the company of the *Flounder*, we held various drills. We went to battle stations surface, fired all guns at a home-made balloon target, and made several training dives. The skippers of each submarine made practice periscope runs on each other, giving the battle stations team tracking practice and the lookouts a chance to view an attack periscope. Later, during darkness, radar attack practice runs were made.

On August 8, 1944, the *Flying Fish* and the *Flounder* arrived at the Admiralty Islands, which had been wrested from the Japanese just months earlier, and moored alongside the submarine tender, *USS Eurayle*, for topping off with fuel.

The next day, escorted by two surface vessels, and in the company of the *Flounder*, we headed toward our war patrol area. The *Flounder's* war patrol would be somewhere in the area of our own.

In cooperation with that submarine, we continued to hone our skills with repeated drills as we proceeded to our target areas. On the second day at sea, the captain informed us that we would be patrolling an area south and east of Mindanao. This was meaningless to me. I had never heard of Mindanao before and had little knowledge of the Philippine area. Matt's response to the skipper's announcement was, "Good place to get some decent shooting." Then, almost as an afterthought, "Good place to get killed."

The *Flounder* had her own orders and we parted company.

On August 14, 1944, we were on station and hunting. The seriousness of our responsibility and position was reflected in the total intensity of my more experienced shipmates.

Chapter 5

Rescue Mission

On station off Manado, we no longer had the luxury of changing locations appreciably. Nor did we have the option of remaining submerged during the daylight hours to avoid exposure. Around the clock, lookouts and radar scanned the sea and the sky for any sign of the enemy or for one of our planes in trouble. The radioman constantly listening for the call of MAYDAY.

A lookout is instructed to report anything unusual. It is not for the lookout to take time for evaluation, that is for the more experienced and better-trained minds to do. While approaching our previous patrol area, I, as a lookout reported smoke on the horizon. This generated considerable excitement. It would have been nice to encounter a lone steam-driven freighter. The "smoke" was a whale spout. The spout was a great distance away. How was a farm boy, fresh from a coal mining region of Pennsylvania to know what a whale spout looked like?

Then, two days later, I reported a periscope sighting. A periscope within shooting range during the war years would strike fear in the mind of any sailor. I didn't take time to evaluate my sighting, but as soon as I gave the report I realized that there was no wake associated with the object. During both my erroneous reports the skipper had the bridge. After a quick look through his binoculars he said, in a voice showing some disgust, "That's a mop handle you see." The wet, heavy mophead, below the surface with several inches of handle pointing straight up, exposed above the surface of the calm water. I was embarrassed, both by my faulty report and by Commander Risser's tone of voice. I mumbled to myself, "That's gratitude, you son-of-a-bitch." I wondered how long that mop had been in the water and if any other vessel's lookout had ever mistaken it for a periscope. Later, as I passed him in leaving the bridge Commander Risser said, "Good work. You have sharp eyes." That necessary balm soothed my minor wound.

Two months later I was promoted and advanced to the rating of Torpedoman Third Class. With that promotion I was given other duties and was a lookout less often. I preferred to think I was promoted because I was deserving, and not because the skipper's heart couldn't take anymore.

A submarine is not equipped to daringly remain on the surface with the enemy nearby. Submarines are not designed to carry the necessary guns for serious surface battle. This assignment was not our choice of duty but it needed doing. Lifeguard duty did not preclude the sinking of enemy ships, and we were constantly hunting as we covered the northeast area of Manado.

We worked our assigned area, hunting targets suitable for torpedo attack or gunfire. There was the possibility that the Japanese would move a Naval Force in against our Task Force, which commanded the air strikes. One night, we made an attack approach on a radar target which looked to be a small ship. Much to the embarrassment of our skipper, it was a high pile of sea weeds. Twice we frightened natives in small fishing boats when we approached their craft to make sure they were natives, and to scan their cargo. The brief event is given below, in the captain's words, as taken from the declassified ship's patrol report:

"They were flying a white flag and doused the sail as we approached. Eleven frightened natives sat still as mice as we circled them. These were very poor people. We traded some rice for a few bananas."

Most of the submarines had an opportunity to respond to the call of MAYDAY at least once. They had the satisfaction of making a concerned, if not scared, young pilot a very happy person. Future President George Bush was one of those pilots. He was plucked out of the sea by the *Finback*, which was on station not far from our location. We on the *Flying Fish* did not rescue any pilots. But we did have exciting moments.

At least once each day and night an enemy plane would force us to dive. We would remain submerged for a short while and then again resume our surface duty. We in the forward torpedo room named the Japanese pilot "Hopeful." We began to accept him. He didn't concern us much; he was very predictable. Usually we had him on radar when he was about seven miles away. Each time a plane contact was made coming from his direction, on a direct course for us, someone would say, "Here comes Hopeful again."

One night I was on lookout during very foggy conditions. I didn't even hear a plane before I saw a bright flash about 200 yards away. Soon after, I heard the explosion. This was the second night of bombing since our arrival. We concluded that the pilot was directed to us by shore radar. It didn't seem likely that a small plane would have radar. If it did, why was the pilot so far off target? We dove rapidly. Probably no need to, Hopeful had dropped his entire load. Radar was relatively new and by today's standards, very crude. Our radar did not pick the plane up through the fog.

Then there was the day our lookouts had good visibility, except for a rain squall building in one small area between us and the direction of the nearest land. I was in my bunk, with the main ventilation system, which ran the full length of the ship, gently blowing air over my upper body. Through the duct I could hear the radarman. His voice came through clearly: "Bridge, pip on radar five miles."

Commander Risser, on the bridge, probably replied, "Very well, keep them coming." That was the usual command, though I couldn't hear his voice.

"Four miles. Three and one-half miles." The orders must have been, "Give me half mile readings." From the radarman, "Three miles Captain. One and a half-mile Captain. Lost pip Captain!" When the plane reached the three mile distance, I was saying, to myself, "DIVE! DIVE!" We seldom waited until a plane came this near at night and never in the daylight hours. Then the dive alarm sounded. Not twice as it should have for a dive, but three times, which was the surface alarm. The skipper, a man of steel nerves, was on the bridge and would have hit the dive alarm. This made it all the more disturbing. As I grabbed the rails of my bunk and waited for the explosion, I could visualize the activity which had taken place topside.

Stretch and the other lookouts on their platforms about five feet above the bridge deck, would respond to the "lookouts below!" command, and make a guided drop onto the deck in one jump. In two or three steps, they would be over the conning tower hatch. Using the ladder rails as guides, in one smooth motion they would drop the seven feet to the conning tower deck, each moving aside to provide a clear and safe drop for anyone who followed. They would reach the control room hatch in two steps and again use the ladder rails in dropping to the control room deck. The watch quartermaster would follow through the conning tower hatch. Last, the captain would drop down the ladder and the conning tower watch officer would slam the hatch shut by pulling on the hatch lanyard. Now the quartermaster who had been hanging on the side of the ladder waiting for the captain to clear, would swing back on the ladder and dog the hatch down. All this in seconds. By the time the hatch was secured, water would be rushing over it.

In the control room directly below the conning tower, the diving officer, at the first blast of the Klaxon (dive alarm) and the shout of DIVE! DIVE!, would have given orders to the diving crew, initiating the dive. Instantly, and in a swirl of action, valves would be opened allowing sea water to flood ballast tanks necessary for attaining proper negative buoyancy. Diving planes would be set and the boat would immediately respond.

We made a dangerously steep dive and didn't level off until we were below 300 feet. No explosion came. Even before we had leveled off, Harding came into the forward room, grabbed a bucket and headed aft towards the crew's head. He didn't respond to our queries of "What happened up there, Stretch?"

Going to the control room to learn what happened would have been unprofessional, so we waited for some word. Soon Stretch returned. This time when questioned he said, "Geez Christ, I shit my pants."

There was a heavy rain cloud at the stern of the ship. This cloud was responsible for the lost radar pip. The lookouts would have heard the communication between the radio room and the bridge. Also, the captain would have cautioned them to greater alertness. As Stretch searched the sky in his sector with the plane's bearing known, the plane burst from the cloud. Stretch said, "That son-of-a-bitch, Hopeful, he broke through that cloud nearly over us, so low I could see his face. I could see two bombs, one on each wing. I know he didn't shoot but I swear, I saw tracer bullets spitting out of his nose gun. Then the bastard dropped those bombs. Geez Christ, you'd have shit your pants too." No one ever kidded Stretch about that event.

Good luck for all of us. Hopeful broke through the cloud too late. He didn't have time to shoot and when he released the bombs he was late with that move also. Momentum carried them past our ship. They landed in the water 15 or 20 feet in front of our bow. Neither bomb exploded. They should have exploded when they hit the water. Had they done so, that would have been it for us. How terrible that would have been, having someone who was just hopeful, do us in. Especially since we had made it so easy for him.[1*]

[1*] After reviewing this portion of my manuscript, "Pete," John Peterman, who remained in the Navy after the war and advanced in rank — a former Lieutenant Commander and an ordnance specialist — offered the following: "Dale, I was the starboard lookout when the Japanese Zero

52

As we pieced it together later, it was a fighter plane, a Zero. It was converted to carry two bombs, one under each wing. The bombs would have been released by manual means. Hopeful came near to being a hero in the eyes of his people.

Why didn't we dive when common practice dictated we should? Three miles had always been our limit. I can only assume that we had picked up a MAYDAY signal previously and felt sure the low flying plane was an American in distress.

With the rescue mission ended, we were disappointed in not having rescued a single pilot, even a little envious of the boats which did. But we were happy to leave. Hopeful or some other Japanese could get lucky.

We had a full complement of fish (torpedoes) and soon had a new patrol area which included the entire east coast of the Philippine Islands, and extended north to the coast of Formosa (now Taiwan). That area had a lot of ship activity. Wherever there was good hunting, there was extra danger from enemy planes and anti-submarine vessels, and that thought was not lost on any of us. This would be the third and final phase of the *Flying Fish's* 11th war patrol.

Proceeding toward our new hunting waters, and sitting on bunks while discussing the rescue mission portion of the patrol phase we had just left, Bennett said, "All in all, that was pretty boring."

Stretch, who was sitting on his bunk at the other end of the room, quietly, but with considerable force,

---

dropped those bombs, and I'm sure his elevation was not higher than my eye level. I could plainly see the pilot. As I recall, the bombs dropped, one on each side of the bow buoyancy tank. Obviously they did not fall far enough to arm the exploding mechanism."

countered: "You wouldn't think it was so damn boring if you were the one who looked into the barrel of that Jap's machine gun!" Then he added, "Skipper was drinking coffee at the time. I'll bet some big fish swallowed the cup."

Matt, grinned, "A shark, I hope. The bastard will have a tough time getting rid of it."

Bennett, his look including all in the room, "Not if it's like the one I saw on the last patrol, Matt." Then for the benefit of us who not been on that patrol he added, "I didn't actually see the shark, but his dorsal fin was as big as one of our bow planes. They grow any bigger they'll be biting our stern off."

Chapter 6

Extending the War Patrol

During the last week of August, 1944, with an adequate supply of fuel and food, and with torpedoes intact, we began extending our hunting northward towards Japan. Our new area included about 1,000 miles of coastline that was controlled by the Japanese. Under the new orders we would work the shipping lanes from the Davao Gulf north to Formosa and many of the port areas in between. After reaching the coast of Luzon, the largest of the Philippines Islands, we would concentrate our hunting in the Luzon-Formosa area.

En route, submerged just off Cape St. Augustin, our sonar operator detected the sounds of a vessel, its sonar equipment searching for propeller sounds or any other sound which would suggest the presence of a submarine. Periscope observation showed the mast of a distant ship. At this early stage of the sighting, only the conning tower officer and the people who heard the sonarman's report were aware of the possibility of a target. The captain was immediately called to the conning tower via a runner. A general announcement would have awakened those sleeping, and created battle-ready excitement in all on board.

Tracking observations gave the general direction

of the ship's intended course. When it became obvious that the ship was moving toward us, the captain changed course to place our boat in an intercept position. At this time, the people in the conning tower and control room were still the only ones with any indication of the present situation and intent. Then — "Battle Stations Torpedo!" "Battle Stations Torpedo!" The announcement came loud and clear, blaring throughout the ship, followed immediately by the continuous gonging of the battle stations alarm.

The battle stations alarm, a sharp demanding sound, alerted all our senses. The previous tranquility of the ship became a flurry of organized activity, as men quickly moved to their battle station positions. The movement through the passageways was fluid, fast, and dexterous. Since the submarine's hull is a tubular structure, headroom is no problem for tall men. Men of medium stature, such as I, were perhaps more comfortable in the cramped surroundings, but not any more efficient. We passed each other in the narrow passageways, brushing as we passed but not changing speed. The oval water-tight hatches between bulkheads (walls or room dividers), about 38 inches high and 22 inches wide, were no obstacle to anyone as we passed through them without changing pace.

All areas of the ship would be manned by men trained to respond with expert efficiency to whatever demands a battle situation might create. The conning tower and control rooms were the command stations, where the course and speed of the target, as compared to our position, would be constantly reported and synchronized. The maneuvering room watch would be standing by to respond to speed change commands. Bow and stern plane operators in the control room would be doing their best to keep the boat at a given depth, allowing the captain minimum periscope exposure.

Bennett was stationed at the forward torpedo room battle phones, and the other experienced people, with Matt as the key person, were standing by the torpedo tubes. The order came to make ready all tubes and open outer doors. Those of us who were least experienced remained in a standby mode as part of the reload crew.

After a long tense period, during which only bits of information came in on the battle phone, the anticipation ended with an order to close the outer doors and secure from battle stations.

What happened up there? Did they change course and get away from us? There was some disappointment in our room, but there was also an expression of relief, and some comments that a small freighter just might not be worth the depth charge attack which was sure to follow. My feelings were mixed. I wanted my first war patrol to be a successful one, but it wouldn't be if we went down after sinking the freighter.

The following is from declassified war patrol records as recorded by Commander Risser:

1445 - Sighted mast of ship. Angle on the bow was nearly zero, so headed towards.

1455 - Can see three ships now - apparently a small freighter with two escorts, one of which is pinging. As escorts are to east of target, changed course to open out to west.

1517 - Made ready all tubes. Something looks fishy here, though. The target can't be more than 1500 tons, is extremely light, has two escorts, and has been on a steady course since sighted. Came to target course to prolong approach, hoping for a zig so I could see just what was going on. The angle on the bow has been too small to afford much identification.

1527 - This looks strange to me. Closed outer doors and went to 200 feet, under a slight temperature break.

1545 - All ships are by. Planed up to periscope depth.

1554 - Target going away on same course. Escorts are both trailing. One is a corvette type with radar, the other is a small SC.

1645 - Ships are now in column, turned east and then north rounding Cape St. Augustin. This surprised me for I felt certain this was a hunter-killer or "bait" group and expected them to stay in the gulf mouth. Hardly know whether to feel good or bad about this incident. It was certainly a borderline case, but I missed a fine chance to test the shallow running qualities of our Mark 23 torpedoes.

1706 - Sighted plane on far side of Cape St. Augustin patrolling north and south over the estimated track of our enemy group.

1735 - Plane turned our way and disappeared in the west.

1949 - Surfaced and stood SSW.

The hunter-killer group was another clever method the enemy was using to lure submarine captains into death traps. At this stage of the war, targets were few, kills were rare, and lures were tempting. This type of trap was known to all submarine captains. Earlier in the war, one submarine luckily escaped after falling for the bait. The lure was a large freighter, probably a patched-up worthless hulk. The game was to let the submarine have the hulk, and immediately attack the submarine with both escorts armed with specially trained crews and the latest weapons for searching out and destroying submarines.

As we continued northward and drew nearer to Japan, small targets were more common, but the protection offered them was even more evident. There wasn't any reasonable opportunity for a gunfire attack. One afternoon, just off Formosa, we spotted a medium-sized freighter with two escorts, but could not get into position without surfacing and exposing our ship. The enemy ships went on their way, not knowing that the few extra miles of distance between them and us meant the difference between life and death.

On the surface we could crank up to 20 knots, (approximately 23 miles per hour). Submerged, our top speed was about nine knots. At that speed, submerged, we would be extremely noisy, and our batteries would be flattened in little more than one hour. Using the batteries with care in an emergency, we could coax 38 or more hours of service out of them. A submarine which was forced down by the enemy, and had a weak battery charge, was in big trouble. After any prolonged period of submerged running, one of the greatest priorities after surfacing was to put one or two of the engines on the generators for a battery charge. There was always the possibility of another forced dive, and additional battery-demanding submerged running.

Aircraft activity was of constant concern to us. The Japanese, with escort vessels and aircraft, were giving their ships, large and small, all the protection they could spare. They had a good right to be concerned. These areas were almost constantly stalked by our submarines, and many Japanese vessels had been sent to the bottom by them. But, for the sinking of those ships, many of our submarines had paid the ultimate price, and several of our boats shared the same watery gravesite as the ships they sank.

The enemy's anti-submarine tactics were both offensive and defensive. Their patrol planes not only worked the shoreline, they ranged out to the open sea, and we were forced down many times. The constant threat was wearing and we were growing tired. We had not seen civilization in nearly three months, and during much of that time we had been under considerable stress.

As we were working the area between Formosa and Luzon, we encountered very heavy seas. One night, we could have submerged and at 100 or 110 feet would have been free from most of the wave motion, but we were in a likely area for successful hunting. If any enemy vessels were out there, our best opportunity for making contact was by remaining on the surface. With the rough seas, if we made contact we could move in with less danger of discovery; so we remained on the surface for a considerable time and were battered by huge waves. At times water splashed over the bridge and some spilled into the conning tower. Unknown to us, the *Flying Fish* was paying a price. As the storm increased in intensity, we dove to the more peaceful area of the ocean.

The worst of the weather passed and we surfaced in the early dawn. Without our knowing it, during the height of the storm, the after portion of the stern deck had been rolled forward 20 or 30 feet.

It looked like a sardine can lid which had been tightly rolled back in the opening process. That section of the stern deck was made from heavy gauge steelplate with perforations in it. The holes were there to allow free passage of water during diving, surfacing, depth charge explosions or heavy storms. Heavy seas should not have been able to do such damage. It was likely that the depth charge attack we had experienced in the Davao Gulf had broken some of the welds. The broken welds were not detected by the relief crew of the *USS Orion*, and the storm had completed the job of tearing the deck completely free at the stern.

The deck looked ugly but the damage could not be considered serious. However, it would impede submerged movement and would be an unwanted noise hazard if we should further need to elude an enemy vessel. Wisdom and common sense mandated termination of the war patrol.

The decision to terminate was greeted with relief and considerable discussion. We were a tired and disappointed crew. Not being able to get into position on the one small convoy was frustrating. We had worked many harbor areas and inlets with no success. Targets were getting scarce. Some submarine skippers were growing bolder and taking greater chances to get at them. Fortunately, the Japanese defensive and offensive weapons were also being depleted.

During a general and light-hearted evaluation of

this third and last phase of the war patrol, Stretch asked Bennett how he rated it. Bennett's tongue-in-cheek response was, "If it hadn't been for those damn planes, I would have slept through the whole thing."

Matt, with a sly look and chuckle, "Other than the planes it was about as exciting as that Aussie girl I shacked up with in Brisbane." I asked Matt to tell us about her. "You wouldn't believe me if I told you."

Stretch grinned, "We know you're going to tell us about her anyway so have at it."

"Well," Matt continued, "The second time we had sex she laid there and ate peanuts the whole time." After the laughter died down Evans asked if she was good looking.

"Not very."

Evans again, "Did she have any good qualities?"

Matt looked surprised to hear the question, "Hell, yes, two. She was willing and available." For a time, the room was filled with laughter.

Bennett, "Pretty hard to top that, Matt. You always put things in the proper order of importance. Will you look her up when we get back to Brisbane?"

Matt, with a look of thoughtful concentration, "No official word yet, but scuttlebutt has it that we won't be going back to Brisbane. About that Aussie girl, the more I think about her, the better looking she gets. If we go back to Brisbane, by the time we get there she'll look better than any pin-up girl."

Stretch, feigning a serious voice, "The solution to the problem is simple. Just don't buy her any more peanuts."

The conversation about Brisbane continued until it ran its course. I thought of Alyce and wondered what my true feelings for her were. In the short time we had known each other we had some good times together. My mind basked in thoughts of our country outing and of our riding rented horses through some of the semi-barren land. Alyce was a nice person. If we did not return to Brisbane our relationship would be ended. I did not even have her address and felt regret about the seemingly unconcerned way in which we had parted.

The light, though raw, nature of the conversation in the room belied the tension pent up in all of us. We had been on patrol a long time with little to show for it. The damage to one freighter which got away was little consolation. The war patrol would go down in naval records as an unsuccessful one, the only un-successful one the *Flying Fish* had ever experienced.

Technically we had been on one continuous war patrol from the time we had left Australia and entered enemy waters, and would continue to be until we reached a home port. The three phases of our war patrol were combined; our brief refueling stop at the tender *Orion* did not constitute a break in the eyes of the Navy. We on the *Flying Fish* viewed it differently. To us it was a brief period of rest and recuperation.

Now it was time to forget the recent past. Thoughts of a home port superseded all others. The home port would not be Brisbane. We were directed to Pearl Harbor. We were beginning to shake some of the tension as we left the enemy waters and thoughts of Hawaii began to enter into our thoughts and conver-sations.

We were a long way from home but our course was set in that direction. With thoughts of danger slowly being erased from our minds, there was no way any of us could have predicted that we would have one more depth charge attack to endure before we reached home port. The circumstances surrounding it were even less predictable.

Chapter 7

'Friendly' Waters, Friendly 'Enemy'

The threatening aircraft and anti-submarine vessels, as well as the depth charge attack, were an unpleasant thing of the past. We were all well, and our boat was still sound. The captain and crew of the *Flying Fish* had outwitted and outmaneuvered the Japanese in all their attempts; and without a doubt, left them in an angry and disappointed state of mind. They were probably still searching the general area, hoping for another chance at us.

This was our third day away from the patrol area. The mental strain and tension had been eased. Our lungs had been cleansed, headaches were gone, and our attitude was excellent. We were running on the surface at three-quarter speed. The day was warm and sunny, visibility was unlimited. The sea was calm. A near-perfect day. Besides, we had just received word that we were scheduled for a refit. Any extensive repair work would require dry-docking in Pearl Harbor and a month or more of rest and recuperation in Honolulu. I had never been to Honolulu and was looking forward to it.

The ship's radio picked up the familiar Asian Broadcasting Station, which featured Tokyo Rose with her sexy and alluring voice. She came on with the usual propaganda about how we were losing the war and how hopeless our efforts were. Again we were told how our wives, girlfriends, and family missed us, and always the question: "Why are you fighting for Roosevelt and the other very rich people in your country?" This in itself was amusing to us, since two of our officers, Lieutenants Chace and Doheny, came from wealthy families. Then she went on to tell all who were listening about the American submarine the gallant Japanese Navy had destroyed just weeks ago in the Davao Gulf. She then named two of our submarines which we knew were patrolling Japanese waters, and informed, "all Americans" that these submarines would never return home, "They will be destroyed just as the one was destroyed in the Davao Gulf."

This was greeted by a range of reactions and expletives. Then a lengthy discussion centered around Tokyo Rose.

Matt pictured her as an American who was the product of marriage between a Japanese Geisha and an American sailor. According to him, she spent most of her life in the United States and gained much knowledge about our Navy from her sailor father. He theorized that when the Japanese were making plans for the war, they solicited her aid and she moved to Japan.

In Bennett's view she was a Japanese-American intellect, educated in our best universities, who turned traitor when the war broke out.

Stretch put it in simple terms: "She was a San Francisco whore who got her information while she was humping our service men and government people." It seemed to Stretch that she would be considered a very special person in Japan and therefore would have a very good life, probably as a mistress of some important general or government official.

The information for the following facts came from: *The Hunt for Tokyo Rose.*

Soon after the war ended there was a hue and cry by those in responsible government positions to bring the traitorous female to justice, and an immediate effort to do just that was launched. After intensive investigation, it was determined that there was no "one" Tokyo Rose. There were many women whom the Japanese forced into that broadcasting position. Most of them were traced down and investigated thoroughly. Only one, Iva Toguri, had not renounced her American citizenship, thereby leaving herself open to prosecution. She was tried for treason, but convicted on a lesser charge and sentenced to serve 10 years in prison.

The evidence against her was questionable, and there was strong evidence that she had been forced into her role of Tokyo Rose. During his presidency, Gerald Ford pardoned her. She had served eight years of the 10-year term.

Conversation turned to the question of whether or not the Japanese truly thought they sank us. Whatever the case, we were satisfied that we had the last laugh. But the concern about their present intelligence gathering was obviously felt by everyone in the room. The fact that they knew the names of those two submarines operating in their waters was disturbing.

The topic quickly changed to hopes and expectations for our return to port and the period of rest and recuperation which would follow. In the past, some of the "old timers" had related exciting tales about their liberties in Honolulu, and I expected to hear more of the same. Strangely enough, the conversation was not at all boisterous, in fact it was subdued, almost as if the paradise we were about to return to dare not be soiled by loose talk. Also, we were a long way from any American port and there was no guarantee that we would get there. The danger was relatively small compared to what it had been just a few days ago, but as was the usual situation with any submarine, we were still alone. This would not change. Submarines did not rate escorts. Besides, we were expected to be able to take care of ourselves.

I could still hear the conversation as I walked down the passageway on my way to the conning tower and my helm watch. These waters were considered ours. There was little danger from Japanese surface vessels or aircraft. But the possibility of a Japanese submarine was always there and we were steering an erratic zigzag course as a precautionary measure. I was in the conning tower, manning the helm and steering the course as it was given to me from the skipper on the bridge, his compass commands coming to me directly through the open hatch. I was relaxed, enjoying my task and the cool fresh air bathing me from the hatch above.

We had some communication about an American Naval Task Force which was moving in a direct line toward us. That armada of war ships was made up of everything from aircraft carriers and battleships down to destroyers and other smaller vessels. The escort vessels, like guard dogs, constantly patrolled the perimeter of the Task Force. The powerful group's only concern was the possibility of a Japanese submarine attack. They would welcome anything else with which the Japanese wanted to test them. They were charged with the responsibility for delivering a telling blow to a Japanese-occupied island. Their course was set and there was no doubting their ability. Soon we began to spot scout planes, and we always gave the proper recognition signal. When the task force came into view, we made contact with them. We gave them our boat's identification and our location, all done in accordance with proper procedure. The Task Force was still a great distance away when we again identified ourselves, and received acknowledgment. Given the distance, with the *Flying Fish* being so low in the water, we may not have been visible to the main body of those ships, but they certainly had us on their radar screens.

I was given a new course to steer, a course which would give the Task Force a wide berth. All was serene as we entered our new course and continued on a direct bearing with no zigzagging. At this time, any enemy submarine in the area would not be interested in attacking us with all those prize targets in the Task Force.

Through the hatch, I could hear isolated words of a conversation between the skipper and the signalman. This was a bit unusual, since speech on the bridge was most always limited to the basic essentials. Then, I distinctly heard Commander Risser say, "They're firing on us!" Almost immediately that was followed by, "Clear the bridge!" and the sound of the dive alarm. It didn't take much imagination to realize what was occurring. One of the advance destroyers was attacking us. With guns blasting and at full throttle she was quickly closing the range.

At that moment Commander Risser was placed in a very difficult position. A ship-saving, life-saving decision had to be made instantly. Any communication with the destroyer would require time and the destroyer's guns would continue to zero in on us as the range quickly closed. If a shell did not strike us, would our identification signal get through? Would all the equipment on our vessel and theirs work properly to insure clear transmission and reception? The skipper had to act on either of two dangerous choices, and elected what he thought was the least dangerous of the two. To remain on the surface without absolute identification meant certain destruction. The destroyer captain was doing the job he was assigned, protecting the fleet against enemy submarines. They certainly must have expected to encounter Japanese submarines. How could such a large force approach so near to Japan without being detected?

Diving would very likely invite a depth charge attack, unless the destroyer's captain chose to use the ship's sonar for an exact location before attacking. If he did so, it would give us time to identify ourselves.

The lookouts came thundering onto the conning tower deck and continued on to the control room. The dive command was never treated lightly, even if done during pre-patrol practice dives. The lookouts seldom knew the exact reason for the dive. On this dive, they too would have seen and heard the gunfire from the destroyer.

Even before the last lookout reached the bridge deck, the Klaxon sounded the diving alarm. Almost instantly, the *Flying Fish* nosed downward. With the signalman prepared to secure the hatch and out of the skipper's way, the conning tower officer pulled the lanyard and closed the hatch as soon as the skipper's head was through it. As the signalman swung back to a position on the ladder in preparation for securing

70

the hatch, water was flooding the bridge and we took on a considerable amount of it. Since I was in a location near and below the hatch, I got an unexpected bath.

The moment the skipper's feet hit the deck, and even before the hatch was secured, he gave peremptory orders, "Take her down to 300 feet, all ahead two-thirds. Rig for depth charge attack!" With little or no pause, turning to me he barked, "Left full rudder, take us to 010!" Then he ordered the conning tower officer below.

In the control room, the diving officer ordered the bow and stern planes set for a steep dive. Almost in the same breath, he ordered flooding of the necessary ballast tanks to make the ship nose-heavy. With smooth efficiency, the Chief Petty Officer who assumed that responsibility, carried through those tasks with great speed.

The force of our surface speed carried through and we instantly nosed downward. The planes cut into the water, and at the same time, the full rudder caused a slanting left turn. It was the steepest dive I had experienced and it was necessary for me to hold tightly to the helm to keep from meeting the deck. The dive was dangerously steep, but the situation warranted it.

From my station on the helm, I was not aware that we had exceeded the 300-foot depth, our boat's recommended maximum, by more than 100 feet before we leveled off. As our boat was being brought back up to 300 feet, the rapidly churning blades of the destroyer's propellers could be heard as the distance quickly closed, making their intentions fairly obvious. They would attack on the first run!

Even as we were diving, the skipper commanded

Roberts, not new to emergency situations, to send the recognition signal. The effort was futile, the destroyer didn't slow down to send out sounding probes or to listen for any communication. We were at one-third speed and on our new course. Roberts continued his signal sending, and we fired an identifying smoke signal.

We could hear the rapid swishing sounds of the propellers. The vessel's speed was steady as it quickly approached. The swishing remained constant, but increased in volume as the destroyer passed very near to our position. Our change in course gave us a margin of safety. Were they making an attack run? Didn't our signaling reach them, did our smoke signal go awry?

Roberts was no longer sending although he still had his headset on. Realizing that the destroyer had dropped depth charges, he grabbed at the headset to protect his ears just as the explosions came. He didn't act in time. My firm grip on the helm kept me in my general position, even though my seat left the stool as the boat shook and rocked as violently as if it had been rammed.

Now the destroyer was sounding on us and the pinging grew stronger. Roberts was attempting to send the recognition signal, but it didn't seem to be reaching the vessel above. Apparently, when he had been thrown from his position, he had inadvertently turned the power off, and with his ears still ringing, he could not know that he was not sending.

There was a dreaded, sinister change in the propeller sounds just as we fired another smoke signal: the tempo of the propeller sounds took on a prophetic air. The vessel had accelerated greatly. The swishing sounds were coming in rapid succession as the propellers moved the vessel above us, away from our location. Like a startled fish accelerating to escape danger, she was rushing forward, quickly distancing herself from us.

"Oh, no! Here it comes again!" It was evident that our attempts to communicate with the destroyer had not been successful. The tempo of the propeller sounds had to mean that more depth charges had been dropped and the vessel was rushing to distance herself from the effects of the explosions. The seriousness of our situation was magnified by the realization that the destroyer had our near-exact location.

A feeling of tension and helplessness permeated the conning tower. The entire boat was probably charged with alarm and the same feeling of helplessness. There was nothing any of us could do at that moment. I glanced at Roberts and the skipper. This time Roberts had removed his headset to protect his ears. Both men were staring in the direction of the propeller sounds above. We braced ourselves and waited out the dreaded seconds.

The explosions came as a continuous and near-deafening series of blasts. The *Flying Fish* lurched, listed, and shuddered. The helm was torn from my grasp and I was thrown across the conning tower deck. The skipper had been thrown against the farthest bulkhead. He was in a sitting position. I was prone, my body over his legs. Roberts was kneeling not far from the sonar, his hands over his ears, his forehead pressed against the bulkhead.

Even before he propelled himself to his feet the skipper was shouting, "Roberts, give the recognition signal! Give the recognition signal!" Roberts remained frozen in his kneeling position. I went back to the helm but I ignored it, partly because I could see no need for steering an exact course under the circumstances, but mainly because I was concentrating on the life-threatening drama unfolding before me. I remember saying, "God, I hope he remembers the signal." Our lives hinged on immediate and proper action by Roberts. There was nothing I could do to urge him into action.

The destroyer was sounding on us. The skipper continued to shout at Roberts, "Give the recognition signal!" At the same time he was slapping and pushing him toward the sonar gear.

Roberts, with a start, almost as if coming out of a deep sleep, became alert and bolted into action. Again and again he repeated the recognition signal. At about the same time, we fired another smoke signal.

The propellers above stopped. Soon Roberts translated a message from the destroyer, who identified herself as the *USS Cogswell*. "Sorry, are you damaged?"

Our skipper replied, "I don't think so."

From the Cogswell, "Come on up."

"Go to hell, we'll wait until you're gone."

Further communication revealed that the destroyer was having difficulty receiving our signals clearly, perhaps because she was directly above us and her propeller noise was causing interference. Then she moved away.

The executive officer, Julian Burke, popped his head through the control room hatch, made a quick visual evaluation and dropped back down.

The skipper asked for a ship's damage report, which when given compartment by compartment, was negative. He then ordered a depth of 90 feet. My compass heading showed 040 degrees. I said, "Damn, they knocked us 30 degrees off course!"

The skipper, being the good leader he was, said rather sharply, "Get back on your course." Then he ordered me to the course we were steering before our encounter with the Task Force.

We secured from silent running but remained submerged for what I considered to be a long time, probably 20 minutes or more. During all that time, except for one small course-change command, no word was spoken in the conning tower.

The duty stations were not changed, and Commander Risser remained in the conning tower. It is reasonable to assume that this command post would be the most comfortable place under the circumstances. He, Roberts, and I were the only ones in the conning tower, and just minutes ago had shared a moment of "life or death" not experienced to such a detailed and intimate degree by any other members of the *Flying Fish* crew.

The second salvo of depth charges had exploded dangerously close to us. During preparations for surfacing, we found that neither periscope could be raised, and that a forward ballast tank had been damaged. After several attempts, the observation periscope did respond, but then it could not be lowered.

After leaving the helm and returning to the forward torpedo room, I was surprised to hear comments by my more seasoned shipmates, who considered the depth charge attack, although of short duration, to be the most serious they had experienced. The damage caused during our brief negative encounter with one of our own destroyers was more grave than that resulting from the recent and prolonged pasting we had taken from the Japanese destroyer.

In addition to the damaged ballast tank, the conning tower and periscope housing had been knocked out of alignment. The extent of the damage compounded the need for repairs. The major repair needs mandated a change in overhaul yards, and we were directed to the San Francisco area. I would not get to see Honolulu this time. Although we would stop briefly at Pearl Harbor for refueling, we would not get shore leave. This didn't concern me. I was concentrating on San Francisco and a 20-day leave for a visit with my family.

As we proceeded on our home course, I wondered why we suffered the depth charge attack. Was it an occurrence which never should have happened? There wasn't much doubt about that, but then, there probably never was a war where friendly fire has not taken lives. Several months before this traumatic experience, an Australian aircraft pilot had seemed reluctant to break off his attack approach on us. This was after we had given the recognition signal several times.

What went wrong? Who was at fault? I was tempted to research this incident through naval records, but I concluded that there would be three or more versions of this. One would come from the Task Force, one from the *Cogswell,* and one from the *Flying Fish.* These would be compiled in a neat and brief summary. Everybody would be covering his own tracks and the Navy Department would have no inclination to expose its own error.

I could write several possible scenarios explaining this near tragedy. Each of the scenarios would have elements of truth, but the total story will never be known. Perhaps that's as it should be.

NOTE: on submarines, quartermasters and signalmen stood the same watch.

Chapter 8

Stateside Bound

On the remainder of our trip to Pearl Harbor, the ocean seemed to know our need for a quiet, restful period and cooperated. We continued our duties in seriousness, but the intensity was not as great; and admittedly, our stressed-out minds were not as capable.

From a distance, the Island of Oahu is a beautiful sight. I likened it to a colossal haystack completely covered with vegetation after being left standing untouched in a spacious meadow for several years. ("You can take the boy out of the country, but you can't take the country out of the boy.")

We were met by two escorts and now everyone seemed to relax. There was a seemingly steady stream of crew members asking permission to come topside. Bridge space was limited and the deck officer kept the movement rotating, with no more than two or three extra people there at any time. As we closed the distance between us and the island, the true beauty stood out even more strongly. I soaked up the tranquil pastoral scenes, with grazing cattle, and cultivated crops growing near the beach.

When we neared the docks, the hatches to topside were opened and the crew members not on maneuvering duty were allowed on the main deck. When the three hatches, those over the torpedo rooms and the one over the dining area were opened, fresh air seemed to rush at us, almost as if it had been waiting for the opportunity. Those hatches had not been opened since we left the submarine tender, *Orion.* Before going topside, Pappy said, "I think I can smell pine-apple."

Evans topped that with: "All I can smell is per-fume."

As the *Flying Fish* approached the dock, we were greeted as if we were royalty. We didn't get the gun salute but we docked to the lively music of a Navy Band. Many high-ranking officers and a great number of other naval personnel stood at attention in a salute to the *Flying Fish* and her crew. This was a proud moment for those of us who experienced it for the first time.

With the boat tied up at the dock and the gang-plank brought over, our key officers stood ready to receive the top brass as they came aboard. The for-malities didn't take long. Then for awhile, there was a steady stream of men coming over the gangplank with supplies. Then friends came on board to greet former shipmates.

A large sack of mail was brought over from the dock, along with boxes of fresh fruit, vegetables, milk, and ice cream. After "Mail Call," I looked up from my reading to see Pappy with a partially eaten apple in his lap, a container of milk on the deck next to him, the remainder of a pineapple slice in one hand, and a letter in the other. Evans, seated next to me as we read and ate, nudged me with his elbow, then: "Pappy, you didn't get any ice cream."

Pappy's mouth was nearly full of pineapple, but

he managed, "Don't worry, I'll get my share later."
We had not seen fresh food for a long time. Our supply was exhausted before we refueled at the *Orion*. The *Orion* treated us to ice cream, but no fresh rations. Today I wonder how much of our craving for those foods was physiological and how much was psychological. On the *Flying Fish* we did not have any vitamin supplement, but we did have adequate meals. Near the end of the patrol, we were eating a lot of canned stuff; the meat and other staples in the freezer had freezer-burned. Also, they seemed to have taken on some of the boat's unpleasant odors, and probably did, since the freezer was opened often during meal preparation. But the craving was there: a feeling I had never felt before and haven't since.

It was October 22 when we arrived at Pearl Harbor. It had been 83 days since we left Australia. This made the eleventh war patrol of the *Flying Fish*, one day shorter than the longest in submarine history.

Our stay in Pearl Harbor was brief. We were there long enough for refueling and for Commander Risser to give the necessary reports to his superiors. Since there was no liberty given anyone there was no need for us to receive the pay we had accumulated. None of us minded, we were San Francisco bound. Pappy got his pineapple, but Evans' "perfume" was about one week away.

Chapter 9

Stateside Sailor

Feasting our eyes on the Golden Gate Bridge and San Francisco on November 1, 1944, we made our way slowly to the Hunter's Point Shipyard. A small band greeted us with rousing music and, as usual, a group of top-ranking officers was there for the formal recognition, but the greeting was not of the same magnitude as the Pearl Harbor reception. There we were honored; here we were acknowledged.

A small sack of mail was brought on deck and distributed. No fresh food came in over the gangplank. We were not returning directly from a war patrol; we were coming from Pearl Harbor. The base mess hall would be available to us. As Matt, I, and several others stood on deck near the forward torpedo room hatch, he said, "I hope San Francisco gives us a better welcome." We were satisfied to be back in the U.S.A.

With pillowcases full of soiled clothing, we left our boat in the hands of the Base Relief Crew and were transported the short distance to the barracks that were to be our temporary quarters. Although there were less than 70 of us, we were given the entire first floor. Many members chose not to stay on the base and rented apartments in San Francisco. The few who were lucky enough to have homes nearby moved back into their pre-navy rooms. We were required to assemble for roll call each morning, but few other restrictions were placed on us. A few days after we were established in our new quarters, we were granted a 20-day leave. Short-notice air transportation was nearly impossible, and those of us who lived a great distance away spent about half of our leave time on trains and buses. Service personnel occupied at least one-third of the trains' seats and I don't remember seeing any vacant ones.

It was so nice to see family members again, and to feel their immediate presence and sincere love. I was treated to my favorite foods and pampered.

During my first evening home, my father and I sat in front of the large global map which he kept in the living room. Mother sat several feet from us with two of my sisters who lived nearby. They listened intently as we discussed the war situation. I had much catching up to do. The interior of a submarine is a very isolated place, deprived of all news.

Father asked my opinion of the overall scheme of the submarine in the war. This gave me a good feeling. I left home knowing that in his eyes I was a boy; now I was being treated as a man. Since there had been no mail from me in three months, he knew that I would have been at sea, and asked if my submarine had experienced a depth charge attack. I answered briefly and guardedly, being careful not to breach what I thought might be security restrictions. As I was relating the experience, Mother left the room. When she returned, her eyes were red and her face showed her inner feelings.

Later, Mother brought out a newspaper clipping

from our local weekly which had portions of the joint letter Martin and I had mailed from New Guinea. We went back to the global map and looked at the Milne Bay area of that island. We discussed the island's importance to our war effort. Until then, they had not known exactly where we had met. If we had mentioned it in the letter it would have been censored out. None of us knew where Martin was, but we assumed he was on another island nearer to Japan. With my finger, I roughly traced our recent patrol route. Again, before I was finished, Mother left the room.

The following day, while Mother and I were alone, she told me how Father studied the map nightly after the news broadcast; and how he pondered and anguished, wondering where his three warrior sons might be and under what circumstances they were living.

My stay was temporary, and didn't make allowance for any comfortable, prolonged period of relaxation. The general environment was not the same as when I left. The embracing little town I left had changed and did not seem to have the feeling of security and protectiveness it once had. None of my boyhood friends were home. They too were in the service. Most of the other young adults had gone to various cities where jobs were plentiful. Defense industries had reached peak production and workers were in high demand. Women were being hired and trained for relatively high-paying jobs which would not have been considered women's work before the war years. There were many "Rosy-The-Riveter" women filling vital gaps in demanding jobs directly related to the needs of our combat forces.

With the changes, our little town was even more quiet and peaceful than it had been, but it was also a lonesome place. I was not the same person and our little town was not exactly a sailor's liberty delight. Still, it was difficult to leave my parents and other family members when the short leave ended and once again I was on the slow train heading back to the West Coast.

The *Flying Fish* in dry dock appeared to be in a shambles, with men scaling her sides, tearing at her decks and welding on her hull. Strange alterations seemed to be in process and we had no real clue as to what all this activity meant in terms of our future. Below decks, things looked much better. The activity and the work in progress was more on a professional scale and for the most part, it was work which we understood. Engines were being overhauled, valves throughout the ship were being checked, and in general, the interior was being inspected and cleaned up. It was evident that something unique was planned for the *Flying Fish* and those who served on her.

During my absence, the usual number of personnel transfers were made. Roberts was transferred. I don't know if the transfer was initiated by Roberts, if his degree of expertise was needed elsewhere, or if Commander Risser acted because of the friendly "enemy" incident. One of the transfers was of direct importance to those of us in the forward room. Larson, a likable and very reserved Second Class Torpedo Man who usually assisted Matt during torpedo firing preparations, was replaced by Torpedo Man First Class Gerald Canaday. Canaday, a good looking, extremely well proportioned, intelligent, and seemingly well-read man, was an outgoing, charismatic individual who fit in immediately. Matt had been promoted to Chief Torpedoman. It was obvious that our Captain had more demanding and important plans for Matt. Canaday would be groomed to assume command of our room. One other addition to our crew added to the scuttlebutt about our next war patrol. He was Francis R. Birkner, Photographer First Class. He would make the patrol with us. This was not a usual thing on a submarine. Something big had to be in the making.

Life became a routine of working on the *Flying Fish* during duty hours, with one-third of our crew working in rotation. This continued on a 24-four hour basis, seven days a week. Our crew took over most of the work previously done by the relief crew, and with the exception of the new installations or alterations, we were doing all necessary overhaul and repair. Any crew member who during our next war patrol would be directly involved with repair or operation of any new installation, was assigned to some assisting task in the installation, and worked along with the civilian experts. In some cases, the work simply consisted of standing by with a fire extinguisher while welding was being done, but a picture of the total installation would be fixed in the crewman's mind and filed for future reference if the need ever arose. I spent many hours standing fire watch, chipping rust and painting. Slowly the *Flying Fish* began to look healthy again.

Pete and I were drawn closer together as friends and often teamed up for liberty or work. Since our weekends were usually free, we took jobs in a warehouse doing general manual labor. In most industries, even part-time help was welcomed. The job was a nice change of pace from our work on the boat and gave us extra spending money.

As work on the *Flying Fish* progressed, the scuttlebutt was that we were preparing for a special mission through a Japanese minefield. With the progression of the work, it became more apparent that our next patrol run would have something to do with mines. Special sonar equipment was installed.

Our surface firepower was beefed up. The four-inch deck gun was replaced with a more modern, more effective, and significantly more powerful five-inch gun. A 40-millimeter gun was welded in place on the after portion of the bridge deck. Pete and I would become the two who would man and fire that gun. The *Flying Fish* began to take on a neat, clean and deadly appearance.

Sometime during our stay at Hunter's Point, the *USS Cogswell* tied up at a nearby dock. With mixed emotion, I went on board our friendly "enemy." I had no feeling for her, but I wanted to talk to the torpedomen who had manned the depth charge racks while we were on the receiving end. I wondered if I should be angry with them for nearly killing us, or if I should give thanks to them for not doing so.

They told me how excitement of battle had dominated their feelings, how eager they were to destroy the "Japanese" submarine below them, and how they hurled curses in our direction as they set the depth charges to explode at a depth of 200 feet. Several commented on how uncomfortable they felt when they learned that they had depth-charged an American submarine. Most of them mentioned how concerned they were that some of us might have been injured. Submarine duty was dangerous enough without them contributing to that danger! We managed to part as friends.

Surmises about our future patrol were rampant. Any unintended leaks of information would have been considered dangerous by the naval authorities, but our speculations had a positive side. We were semi-prepared when the true facts became known. In a way, the speculation heightened enthusiasm for many of us. There was considerable apprehension, but this was overcome by the exuberance of youth. There was the thought of a daring adventure and the opportunity to strike some telling blows and, in a way, avenge our country.

With the *Flying Fish* spick-and-span throughout, we made our way under the Golden Gate Bridge and on to San Diego and to that Naval Yard, where additional and special sonar equipment was installed. This sophisticated equipment would make it possible for us to detect mines as we approached them while submerged. Or, as Matt put it, "That's what they're supposed to do according to those experts, but you notice none of those experts is going to make the next patrol run with us. Probably just as well, chances are they'd screw up and get us killed."

With our boat's crew members who would man the new equipment thoroughly trained and comfortable with it, we made daily trial runs, testing, adjusting, and re-testing as we worked our way through dummy minefields. Some of the shore experts were with us on those trial runs, and they assisted our sonarmen until their skills were finely honed.

When our skipper and the experts felt that we were ready, we began stocking the boat. Once again, food, fuel, fresh water, spare parts, torpedoes, and ammunition were brought aboard. We headed for Pearl Harbor, where still more work was scheduled for our boat. None of the crew had any exact knowledge of our next war patrol. Speculation in the forward torpedo room had us teaming in a Wolf Pack and making an offensive attack on the remaining Japanese war ships, which were somewhere in hiding, waiting to oppose any attempted invasion of their mainland. Then the guessing began as to where we would find them. Would they be in some big harbor, and if so, where? And what was the purpose of the photographer? Were we going to cozy up to the shoreline to get photographs which would give our military experts information about possible landings for an invasion?

Getting into a harbor was one thing, and probably achievable with our mine-detecting equipment. Getting out was the big problem. Most harbors had shallow water with difficult under-water maneuverability. Once we fired on ships and made ourselves known, our chances of exit would be slim to none. Surely we were not going on a suicide mission. What then, was our plan?

The waiting and guessing was not new to any of us. Information about any impending war patrol was always a tightly-kept secret. I accepted the position of the soldier — "Ours is not to question why; ours is but to do or die." The thought of dying seldom crossed my mind; I was young and feeling invincible.

Chapter 10

Back to the War Zone

Our stop in Pearl Harbor was strictly for business. There was much to be done and no liberty was granted, but two-thirds of the crew were permitted to enjoy the relative luxury of the base, while one-third stood watch on the boat and a base relief crew worked on it. One antenna was replaced and an additional one of different type and purpose was added. But the telling addition was the installation of mine cable clearing protection around the bow planes, stern planes and the propellers.

In forward torpedo room discussion, I questioned the wisdom of the naval top brass and asked, "Why didn't we have all of this done when we were in one of the other two dry docks?" Bennett and Matt both responded.

Bennett: "Both of those dry docks have ships stacked up and waiting. They sent us to one that isn't quite as swamped."

Matt, adding to that, said, "That may be part of it, but I'm inclined to think that this installation was done here to get it far away from any spy's eyes. There's no doubt about the purpose of those cables. The only question is where and when they will be needed."

The *Flying Fish* and her crew had a schedule to keep, with several other submarines waiting for us. So, contrary to regulations, the naval top brass put us into dry dock with a full load of torpedoes and ammunition. Most of the crew was on the base. I was standing room watch in the forward torpedo room. Welding was to be done on the outside hull in the area of the forward torpedo tubes. To protect against the minor danger of heat buildup in the two lower tubes, we pulled the torpedoes about halfway out, and left them half on the reload rack, and half in the tubes. However, before that could be done, the torpedoes normally occupying those racks as reloads had to be removed. They were placed in chocks on the topside deck directly above the torpedo room.

The repairs were being made; the welding was in progress. I was alone in the torpedo room, wearing earphones, in charge of and responsible for that room. It was boring duty and I was in a state of near-total relaxation. All was quiet and serene when, without any warning, an ABANDON SHIP! ABANDON SHIP! ABANDON SHIP! announcement was made over the phone and over the boat's general communication system. This was followed immediately by the continuous death-awakening blast of the proper alarm. That alarm, when sounded, demands instant action. I had never heard the order before, few sailors ever do. I had heard the alarm briefly during test periods.

Within my limited view, I could see no person or activity. The first thing that came to mind was a battery explosion, but there was no indication of that, no fumes were evident. There was no unusual noise, no sudden vibration, or other movement of the boat. Standing nearly below the open hatch, once more I looked through the bulkhead hatch toward the control room, but got no hint of any problem. There was no telling sign, no odor, no smoke. None of my senses were bringing a message to me. Completely baffled, with my concerns gearing to the jolting effect of the sounding alarm, I removed the headphones and started up the ladder. As my head came over the hatch-lip, I saw flames licking up over the ship's deck, extending several feet above the deck and above the two torpedoes resting on it. Smoke was billowing high into the air.

As my mind raced, trying to evaluate the situation, weighing the circumstances and seriousness of the danger, I paused for a moment viewing a scene of total contradiction. The danger was obvious. The confusing sight was the throng of sailors lined up at the dock's railing watching the flames and the efforts of the dry dock firefighters, which were not visible to me. The sight of the flames near the topside torpedoes should have been enough to scatter the onlookers, who may not have known that we were fully loaded with torpedoes and ammunition. It didn't take any reasoning to know why these onlookers were, position-wise, no better off than those of us on the boat if an explosion occurred. The obvious topside danger should have been disturbing to all who were viewing the flames. If a torpedo exploded, the entire boat would become one massive bomb. The torpedoes on deck did not concern me as much as the two below just halfway out of the tubes. The area around those tubes would be the central point of the fire. The tar-like substance used to coat submarines for protection against the salt water was especially thick on the hull in that area, and that substance burned at a high temperature.

With the exception of the forward room crew, the

91

conditions of those torpedoes below were known to very few. The majority of the boat's crew rarely entered the forward room. The boat's "front door," or main hatch, was directly above the dining area. It was near the crew sleeping quarters and the dining room was also the recreation room. Despite the location of the officers' quarters, between the forward room and the control room, even they usually used the dining area hatch.

During the brief pause at the hatch lip, I observed several sailors hurriedly making their way over the gangplank. There was other activity, with two people coming toward me from that same gangplank. Just as I raised my shoulders above the deck, a foot was placed on my shoulder. Lieutenant Eric Hopley, who was our Torpedo and Gunnery Officer, and Matt were standing over me. Lt. Hopley said, "Let's get those torpedoes back into their tubes." Even if I had not agreed to the decision, I had little choice. He and Matt were coming down. I dropped to the deck wondering how hot those tubes had gotten by this time. I'm sure that we were all thinking that the safest place for them was in flooded tubes. A special tank of water is stored for the purpose of flooding the tubes prior to opening the outer doors and firing.

A torpedo weighing 2,800 pounds does not handle easily, and the loading process demands mechanical means. With it partially in the tube and partially on the tube rollers, the toughest part was done. During reload, after the torpedo was within a few feet of seating, Matt and I, who were of near equal-size and worked well as a team, would force it the remaining few feet, using only muscle power. The problem before us was compounded since the torpedoes were only halfway home, and the rollers on the racks were not as cooperative as those in the tube. Using the same method, we sat on the rack behind the torpedo, back to back in a crouched position. With my feet braced against the rack, and Matt's against the torpedo, we forced our legs outward. With great effort and three position changes, we forced the torpedo home. As soon as the torpedo hit the stop, Matt jumped off the rack, slammed the door shut, spun the door lock, and opened the flood valve. I was in position waiting for him on the second torpedo rack. While we were forcing that one into the tube, water began hissing into the bilges indicating that the first tube was flooded. Lieutenant Hopley closed the flood valve and stood by to open the one on the second tube. We did not flood any of the remaining four tubes which contained torpedoes. Our thinking was that they would be protected from the heat by those bottom tubes we had flooded. Less than one minute after flooding the second tube, while Matt and I were catching our breath, word came that the fire was out.

From the time the abandon ship order was given, without having knowledge of the total picture, I experienced fear which I had never known before. During a depth charging, the enemy was known and we all had a pretty good idea of what to expect. As we forced the torpedoes into the tubes I visualized the possible explosion with parts of the *Flying Fish* passing over Honolulu. Later the crew discussed the incident more than was usual. Normally, unpleasant happenings were not discussed in much detail. Finally, Canaday summed it up as: "Much ado about nothing," with an "all's well that ends well" attitude which we all accepted.

While the dry dock work was being completed, Pete and I were assigned to the 40-millimeter gun.

With our gun crews, along with the men who would man the five-inch gun and their gun crews, we were transported to a target range for a day of instruction and practice firing. Both Pete and I were familiar with guns of various kinds, for we had both hunted game and it was easy to adapt to the 40-millimeter gun. Our team was given high marks, and I felt comfortable with my added responsibility.

The work scheduled for our boat had been hurried but well done. We departed San Diego on April 29, arrived at Pearl Harbor on May 5, and the *Flying Fish* had been quickly put into dry dock. Several days later with all the work completed, and with much speculation about our final destination, we left Pearl Harbor and headed for the Island of Guam where the Submarine Tender *USS Holland* would become the base of operation for our short stay.

Some voyage repairs were required on the *Flying Fish* when we arrived at the *Holland*. The *Holland* relief crew took care of those. We, the *Flying Fish* crew, had other business. Soon after reaching the *Holland*, the gun crews went ashore for more gunnery practice. During these practice sessions, most of the shooting Pete and I did was at a radio-controlled drone plane, a serious but enjoyable activity. We did our best to blow the target out of the sky, without success. It was a small target, at a great distance, and the person or persons operating it were very careful of the expensive target. Several days later we practiced with all the boat's guns, firing on a tug-towed target.

Some of the members of our crew voiced curiosity, if not concern, about the role the guns would play in our near future. With the five-inch gun propelling a projectile five inches in diameter, and about 16 inches long as rapidly as it could be manually loaded, we had surface firepower. Add to that the 40-millimeter gun, with its projectile more than one and one-half inches in diameter, and about eight inches in length, which was fired at the rate of one per short second, with our loader constantly replacing ammunition clips. The *Flying Fish* now had more fire-power than most freighters carried.

It was not a practice of submarines to challenge freighters to gun-battle duels. Although submarines presented a low profile target, with that as an advantage against a surface ship, a surface ship could take many hits. Any direct hit on a submarine would cause serious damage and could be its undoing. We accepted the fact that those guns were there in case we needed them. We looked upon them as a form of insurance.

Ours was one of nine submarines using the *Holland* as a temporary base. The possibility of a wolf pack attack on some group or groups of enemy ships became an accepted rumor. For several days we made practice runs, operating in groups of three with the *Flying Fish* leading the *Bowfin* and the *Tinosa*. Now the wolf pack rumors seemed factual. Were there separate groups of Japanese ships in hiding which we would attack as wolf packs of threes, simultaneously?

In a state of battle readiness, we made our way toward the Japanese mainland. We still had no official information on our intended destination or purpose. This knowledge was guarded by the two people who had to know, Commander Risser and his second in command, Lieutenant Commander Julian Burke, the executive officer. In the event of capture en route, none of us would be able to give the enemy any specific details about our intent. This was understood and accepted, it was the usual thing. Even the boat's captain did not have specific details of a relatively routine war patrol until he opened his sealed orders near the patrol area. The nature of this war patrol demanded thorough knowledge of all details, which could have been made known to our captain as early as our San Diego training period. We would be entering new waters with questionable charts and many unknown factors. We would take things as we found them and adjust to the situation's demands.

One day away from Guam, we came upon a floating mine which had broken away from some anchor cable. This type of mine: a sphere full of explosives, and about three feet in diameter, its exterior covered with many spine-like projections. The bases of the projections were fitted with minor detonation charges just waiting for some ship to strike and trigger them. It provided some more gunnery practice for all of the gun crews. Rifle fire and 50-caliber machine guns caused the mine to smolder for a short while. Three shells from the five-inch gun were very near target, attesting to the accuracy of those gunners. Then, Pete and I blew it out of the water with our 40-millimeter gun. Later that same day we came upon another stray mine. The 50-caliber gun took care of that one. Those mines had broken away from their anchor-cables and were a definite navigation hazard. I wondered how many more were out there, and what the chance would be of a ship striking one in the darkness of night.

We had covered about half the 1,600 miles to the Japanese mainland when we picked up a distress signal from one of our bombers. The bomber, returning from a bombing raid on Tokyo, had suffered considerable flak damage. We moved into an intercept position but could not locate it. The *Tinosa* informed us that they spotted the life raft drop, and that they had a bearing on its location. She picked up ten crew members and later transferred them to a submarine which was on lifeguard duty in the area.

We were several miles from the Tsushima Strait when a gray dawn began to break, outlining the land mass before us. We submerged with batteries fully charged. Our skipper spoke to us over the boat's speaker. His comments were brief and to the point. He was a matter-of-fact, dependable man of much courage and few words: "We are nearing the Tsushima Strait. We're going to do what we've been trained for. We are going through that strait and into the Sea of Japan; then we will take care of business."

He didn't say any more. It was imperative for us to remain undetected until we chose to make ourselves known to the enemy. He knew and trusted his crew. Cautioning us against any unwanted activity would have been a minor insult.

In a state of concern but acceptance, realizing that a minefield lay before us, I came off watch, stripped to my underwear and climbed into my bunk.

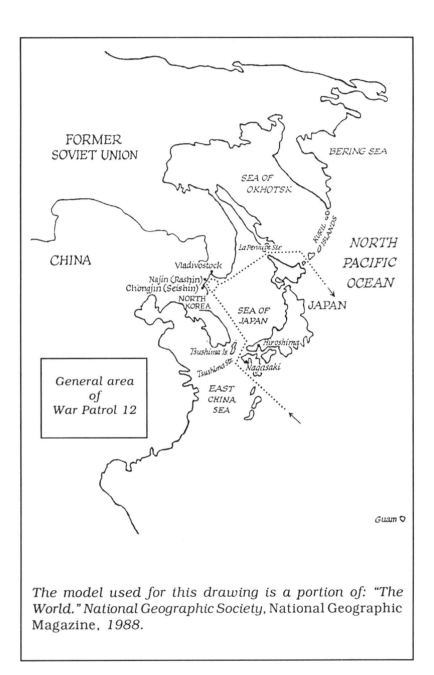

The model used for this drawing is a portion of: "The World." National Geographic Society, National Geographic Magazine, 1988.

The Flying Fish *Prepared for War Patrol 12*

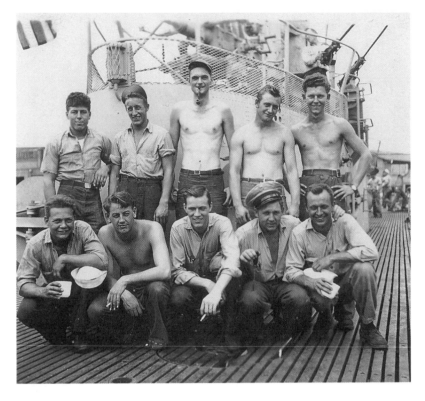

Most of the Crew from both Torpedo Rooms

Left to Right - Upper Row

Dale Russell
Harold E. Holloway
Raymond D. Sproull
Gerald B. Canaday
Glenn E. Ragsdale

Left to Right - Lower Row

John J. Peterman
Cassel J. Evans
Wilfred A. Bennett
John W. Mattingly
Joseph S. Kocon

Chapter 11

Hirohito's Private Bathtub

The rasping, grating sounds jolted me out of my sleep. I sat up abruptly, my sleep-heavy mind trying to evaluate the possible danger. The sound stopped. I thought, 'The damn thing is snagged!' I could visualize the mine floating above us attached to its steel anchor cable, quickly being pulled toward our boat's deck. Then a thumping sound as the cable came free and continued its scraping down the length of our ship. This was the first mine anchor-cable we had brushed. But we still had several more hours in these waters. How many more would greet us in this way? Would they all slip by?

Bennett had the forward torpedo room watch. He and I were the only two awake in the room. Our eyes met, then we both looked toward the ominous sounds. No word was spoken. Each of us waited for the other to speak. Then as Bennett turned away, I, being aware of the others sleeping, quietly said, "Wake me when it's time for my watch … if we're still alive."

I lay back on my bunk. The scraping sounds were gone. I wondered if we had passed the cable or if it was just now passing the after torpedo room? How much time should that have taken? I started to calculate, "Let's see, we are making two knots, and the boat is

312 feet long. I'll need to convert knots to miles per hour and change the boat length from feet to a mile fraction. There are 5,280 feet in a mile. The final result will need to be in feet per second. Oh, hell! Too damn complicated. Not worth the effort."

Without realizing it, I was growing into a seasoned and hardened warrior. Few on board the *Flying Fish* had illusions that the justice of our cause would protect us from harm. Each time we came back to port, we learned of other submarines which did not return. No one knew better than we did that submarine duty was daring and dangerous business. Had we known that our mortality rate was one out of every five, the highest of any branch of our armed forces, I don't think it would have mattered. We had all volunteered for this unique duty. We were physically and psychologically screened before being judged suitable to cope with the rigors of submarine warfare. Also, the *Flying Fish* was our home. She was our lady. Whatever fate had in store for her would be the same for us. A proud vessel, with a proud crew.

The next thing I remember was Bennett's quiet voice telling me that it was time for my watch. Bennett's face had a look of eagerness. His voice was quiet and controlled, but it vibrated with restrained excitement which matched that written on his face. "We're through the minefield and word is that a seaport city is in view. It's unbelievable! They say everything is lit up like Christmas-time back home! City lit up, port lit up, ships have their running lights on! Damn, couldn't we raise hell if we could start shooting!"

Attacking would not be our first priority, even if it had been permitted. To remain undetected, we had dived long before reaching the minefield and had been submerged for nearly 16 hours. Our batteries needed charging and we needed fresh air. The shooting would come later.

At a speed of two knots, moving against the current, we had good steerage and were still able to stop within a short distance when we were on a direct collision course with a mine. Also, propellers turning slowly make little noise. This was very important, since there was a possibility that the Japanese had hydrophones placed in strategic locations as a special precaution against the very thing we were doing. All human activity had to be kept at a minimum. This was to keep the noise down, to conserve oxygen, and to keep the carbon dioxide level as low as possible.

But all of that, along with the minefield, was behind us. A feeling of great relief, mixed with the excitement of anticipated fighting action permeated the atmosphere within the *Flying Fish*. Soon we would surface, circulate fresh air through the boat, collect the spent carbon dioxide-absorbing chemical, and while charging our batteries, head for our designated patrol station. The captain now informed us that was to be the North Korean coast, some 450 miles away. The specific areas of our responsibility were the port of Seishin (now Chongjin), the port of Rashin, (now Najin) and the waters between these two. At times we would be only 15 miles from the Russian border.

I wondered why we were going into the Korean waters when Japan was our enemy. Pappy, his thoughts apparently paralleling mine, spoke almost as if to himself, "Why are we going after the Koreans?"

Canaday, who had knowledge beyond that of most sailors, looked over: "Can that crap, Pappy. Hell, the Koreans have been part of the Japanese Empire for many years, and those ports are probably furnishing the Japs with vital war supplies. Right now they're just as much our enemies as the people living in Tokyo." After a brief pause he added, "But I think we would all rather trade locations with one of the other boats hitting the Japanese mainland ports."

Matt, seemingly disinterested, added: "Depth charges or bombs dropped by Koreans will kill you just as dead as any dropped by Japs."

It was now obvious that none of our nine boats would take part in what would be considered true wolf pack attacks. Instead, each was assigned a specific area, and all the major ports within the Sea of Japan would be hit. If the opportunity for a combined attack on a group of ships came, we would certainly jump at it.

Harold Hollaway, perhaps the youngest member of the ship's crew, was on the helm during the last and most dangerous part of our passage. On orders from the skipper, he guided the *Flying Fish* through the minefield as gently as if she were a baby carriage. Now Harold, nicknamed "Half Hitch" by Matt, was relieved on the helm. (Matt picked up on the H.H., the first day Harold became a crew member.) Harold was training as a torpedoman and was a member of the after torpedo room crew. As Pete, who was in the after room, later related it to me, "He had a big smile on his face as he entered the room. He acknowledged our praise with an even bigger smile as he climbed into his bunk. One deep sigh of exhaustion, — perhaps satisfaction, and he was asleep." Then he added, "I think that during those hours, Hitch made the transition from boy to man."

Information gathered through Naval Intelligence and the newly perfected sonar, which acted like radar under water, plus cables welded as shields around our bow planes, stern planes and propellers, made negotiating the minefield possible. The cables acted to ward off any mine cables we happened to brush. This was a large-scale battle test, the first such test for this new equipment. Our ordnance and intelligence people had bet our lives on the equipment, and on the information they had gathered about the minefield. They wagered the lives of the men in nine submarines. However, the stakes were high enough to justify the wager. An invasion of Japan seemed inevitable. Such an invasion would be costly in American lives. An invasion of Japan could result in door-to-door combat if the Japanese were determined not to surrender. This type of fighting would not only result in the death and injury of many fighting personnel on both sides of the conflict, but it would also ravage the civilian population.

The fact that the Japanese were resorting to kamikaze attacks, and their incredible stand on Iwo Jima suggested that they would be determined to fight "to the last man."

In the kamikaze attacks, young men were trained just enough to fly an aircraft and were sent out against our ships without gasoline enough for a return flight. These were determined young men, willing to sacrifice themselves by diving their craft into a ship.

The stand of the Japanese soldiers on Iwo Jima was equally suicidal. The operation against that island began on February 16, 1945, with heavy bombing. Three days later, assault troops of the fourth and fifth Marine divisions launched a ground invasion. Despite the heavy bombing and shelling by naval vessels of the known gun positions on Mount Suribachi, after our Marines moved up on the beach, those well protected guns opened fire and our Marines suffered heavy losses.

The enemy was dug in and fierce resistance continued. On February 23, 546-foot Mount Suribachi was taken and the American flag was raised over it. (The photograph of the event, although it is a "staged" photo, taken at a later date, is one of the best known of that war.) But the terrible ordeal of destroying the defenders did not end until March 16. Of the 21,000 Japanese on that island, only 216 surrendered. The American casualties totaled nearly 25,000 with 6,800 deaths.

The Japanese resolve, driven by religious fanaticism, had to be broken. The destruction we were charged with inflicting upon them in their seemingly safe and protected waters would surely weaken their will to fight.

The nine submarines slipped through the Tsushima Strait in groups of three, with each group taking a slightly varied route. The *Flying Fish* led one group. Our chosen route through this body of water, with its treacherous mines, was between the island of Tsushima and Honshu, the main island of Japan. Our accomplishment was something obviously thought to be impossible by the Japanese experts. The strait was scanned from ship and shore on radar and undoubtedly by many eyes. What submarine captain would be foolish enough to attempt an underwater passage? The four-layered minefield, with some mines designed to catch submarines at periscope depth, and others set to prevent deep travel, were laid out by experts. How could any submerged submarine travel through that deadly maze without either striking a mine or pulling one down on itself? They should have heeded the old adage which says, "Never underestimate your enemy."

Reports, relayed to us later that day by those who were in the conning tower, described an incredulous Commander Risser as he viewed through the periscope a scene which gave no indication that this part of the world was at war. This was a puzzling contradiction to all which seemed reasonable. We knew that Tokyo had been the recipient of many American bombs. Even if we had doubts about the claims of our Air Force people, we had first-hand reports from several of our submariners who witnessed some of the bombings.

While on Guam, during a rest period, it became common practice for some of our submariners to ride along with the bomber crews during their raids. This dubious form of "recreation" was quickly stopped when word of it got to the submarine captains and other commanding officers.

The periscope view suggested that our bombers were not reaching very deeply inland. This was June 5, 1945, and our war with Japan was nearly four years old. That Japanese complacency was soon to change. Our shooting hour was scheduled for sunset, June 9, less than four days away.

To capitalize on the element of surprise, the chosen attack time was planned to allow for every submarine being at its assigned location with ample opportunity to plan the first attack, have daylight for the shooting, and darkness for retreat and reloading. And while charging batteries, the submarines could be running on the surface to change location, getting into position for a pre-dawn attack in another area.

The lighted city and lighted ships gave proof that the Japanese people were still cocky and not feeling the effects of the war nearly enough. Even America was not that audacious. Our seaports were always blacked out. Unlike Germany, which was within easy bombing range of Allied planes, Japan had not suffered serious and sustained bombing, except for Tokyo. The ports farther inland, especially those bordering the Sea of Japan, had thus far been spared the wrath of our bombers. They almost seemed to be daring anyone to try bombing or invading.

Our task: TAKE THE WAR TO THEM! Sink everything we could by torpedo or gunfire. Shell anything we could. Create whatever havoc we could and generate as much fear and panic as the situation would permit. Finally, we were to instill anxiety, uncertainty, and the realization of impending defeat in the minds of the common people in Japan, as well as in the minds of the military and governing classes. All our efforts would be directed toward bringing about an early surrender. We were not in these waters for the sole purpose of sinking ships and killing the enemy. The Japanese had to know that the waters leading into the Sea of Japan were no longer impenetrable, that there were no remaining safe havens for the Japanese ships, and that their last sanctuary had been invaded. This submarine war patrol would bear psychological fruit for the American war effort.

With great expectations and even greater concerns, we left the Tsushima Strait area. This was an exciting but dangerous venture we had undertaken. What young, hot-blooded submariner would not have welcomed such an opportunity to strike a telling blow at enemy forces in an area where they had not previously felt the retaliation of the angry American people? Sinking ships was the business of submarines; we would be the businessmen.

War had finally come to the "Land of the Rising Sun" in the form of nine deadly invaders. It would be announced by the explosions of 750-pound explosive charges, carried to Japanese ships by American torpedoes when all nine submarines were on station and the synchronized shooting hour had arrived. HIROHITO'S PRIVATE BATHTUB LAY BEFORE US!

Chapter 12

Racing the Shooting Hour

Ours was the last group of three to traverse the minefield. The first group, led by the *Sea Dog*, included the *Crevalle* and *Spadefish*. They entered the strait nearly two days earlier. The *Tunny*, leading the *Bonefish* and *Skate*, followed approximately 12 hours later. After allowing a near-equal span of time, we had poked the nose of the *Flying Fish* into the minefield. But now, the Tsushima Strait with its mines was behind us.

With a safe distance between us, the minefield, and the dimly glowing lights of the port city, we surfaced. We had no communication with any of the other boats, but since we had not heard any massive explosion, they had to be intact and in the Sea of Japan with us. We would not communicate with any of them until after the shooting hour. Nothing was to be chanced. It was to be a total surprise to our enemy. The hope was to be lined up on some fat valuable Japanese vessel when zero hour came. But first, we were in great need of fresh air and a battery charge. These two things took precedence over making rapid progress towards our "hunting grounds."

We surfaced in the teeth of a fierce storm. A very cold wind, blowing from the Arctic, with no regard for the time of year, chilled the rain it gathered as it moved over the Sea of Japan to greet us. Huge waves, generated by the storm, seemed intent upon making it difficult for us to navigate the 450 miles in time to be on station when the shooting hour arrived. As if to test the seriousness of our intent, the wind velocity increased and the sea responded with greater ferocity. Waves crashed over our bow and occasionally sprayed over the bridge.

For those of us below deck, it was not necessary to see the water above to make an a fair evaluation of the topside conditions. The boat was in a condition of constant, harsh motion, with its bow frequently being tossed up above the sea, and then dropped back down with jarring force.

Moving slowly to avoid taking on water, we attended to our most immediate need: charging batteries, as we proceeded toward our northern Korea patrol area.

Four hours later, with healthy batteries, we dove beneath the turbulent sea in hopes of waiting out the storm. Those of us who had not been topside did not get the true picture of the storm. Stretch, who was one of the lookouts, came into the room drenched. His heavy foul-weather clothing offered meager protection against the savage storm and his teeth were chattering as he entered the room.

Matt complained, "With these conditions, we'll play Hell getting to Seishin Harbor before the shooting hour. Hell of a note, a submariner's dream, catching some ship's captain with his pants down and his running lights on, and we'll miss it. By the time we get into shooting position, those Japs will all have the word and will be hiding like rabbits."

Stretch, pulling off his wet clothing, stopped in

the middle of removing his coat, and looked Matt squarely in the eyes. "You'd be bitchin' a lot more if you had to stand lookout duty. Geez, it's cold up there. Colder than a witch's tit." He continued to remove his clothing. "Geez, I thought San Francisco's winter was cold when it was raining and blowing. That's like springtime compared to conditions topside. Damn strange weather for June."

Pappy interrupted, "You don't know what cold is. You should spend a winter in Pittsburgh."

Stretch ignored Pappy, "Deck officer was alone on the bridge. Quartermaster was in the conning tower hanging onto the hatch lanyard. The deck officer yelled at the quartermaster below every time a big one was coming, so he could slam the hatch shut. Deck officer's getting a soaking, but he wasn't as bad off as we were; he had the sprayshield to protect him. Lots of times those waves were splashing around us knee high. Damn glad those batteries are charged!" Then, "You'll get your chance up there Pappy, then you'll know what I'm talking about."

Even at 120 feet the wave motion was evident. The storm seemed to be increasing in intensity. Canaday and I discussed the storm and the possibility of missing the prime shooting time. As Canaday put it, "You'd think that after all we did to meet her, the Sea of Japan would welcome us in a more hospitable way. She's certainly not being a very gracious hostess."

Several hours later, with the storm still raging above, but the crew rested from the ordeal of the minefield passage, we surfaced again and fought our way in a northwesterly direction. Now, I was on a lookout platform experiencing the very thing Stretch had suffered through, and wondering, "What the Hell are we lookouts doing up here? With the black night, howling winds, icy cold rain, and rough sea, only if a near-collision occurs will we be able to see any vessel. Hell, I can barely see our ship's bow when it's not under water. Maybe the glow of a lighted ship can be seen at a distance, or some sound heard, such as a fog horn. So what, even if a Japanese crew spots us, they'll think we're one of theirs. They have no idea we're in their sea."

As I peered into the darkness, I gripped the protective rails with both hands to guard against any extremely large wave. The binoculars hung from a neck-strap; with the constant spray, they were useless. As it was, I frequently wiped the salt water from my face to improve my vision. We were traveling as fast as conditions permitted, but not with the speed necessary to get in on the "virgin shooting" as Canaday put it.

I had been on watch nearly two hours; I was soaked and chilled to the bone. Frequently waves were spraying over me and the other two lookouts, then a big one hit. I was completely underwater, and the wave carried my feet off the platform. My only remaining contact with the boat was the lookout guard railing, and I was hanging on with both hands while the wave dragged at my body. The water's force came very near to breaking my desperate grip on the railing. I was tested to my limit as the wave passed, leaving the boat with a high degree of list. My feet were dangling beyond the lookout platform, there was nothing but the sea below, and I was losing my grip on the slippery railing. In desperation, I was reaching back trying to get my feet back to the platform. Slowly the boat cooperated and started to regain an upright position. As I achieved a position of safety, I noticed the deck officer's face, and it was a face of concern as he looked above to see if he had lost any of his lookouts. He had just replaced Commander Risser, who left the bridge to clean up. Commander Risser left soon after sending a very seasick lookout below. The lookout lost his meal and the skipper was the un-happy recipient of the spray from it. (With my suscep-tibility for seasickness, I went without eating. I was feeling plenty queasy, but controlling my stomach.)

Lookouts were ordered below. Radar would be our eyes, even though there was some question about its reliability under these stormy conditions.

The wave was too big and too fast for the team of the deck officer above and the quartermaster in the conning tower. They did not act rapidly enough, and we took on a lot of water through the hatch. The water sloshed around in the conning tower and then flooded into the control room. Both rooms were treated harshly by the salt water. A submarine's complicated electri-cal system does not take kindly to salt water, and many systems were shorted out. This meant a lot of work for the electrical crew. Under Warrant Officer Bob Emmons, they were capable of almost any repair, and this situation required much cleaning and drying of electrical equipment parts before the Flying Fish was fully functional.

With speed reduced, we suffered less from the force of the waves and continued to make progress; however, it was now a certainty that we would not be in our desired position on time. In the forward room, Matt, lamenting our luck, said, "Some of those boats are already on station scouting things out. Hell, they could go right into a harbor, look things over, then get back out without the Japs ever knowing they were there. They're going to get some good shooting, take their pick. We're going to get the leftovers!" With a look of disgust, "Top brass screwed up; why didn't they give areas farthest away to the first boats through the minefield? They probably didn't even think about heavy seas. Most of them have been on shore so long they don't even remember what heavy seas are like." The one thing that Matt did not take into consideration was the frustrating wait those other submariners experienced. It must have been difficult to pass up perfect set-up shots at juicy targets. All they could do was to make practice runs on them and hope to see them on another day.

I was devoting most of my concentration to keeping my recently-eaten meal down, and it was obvious that I was not alone. Many on the boat claimed to not be troubled with seasickness. These claims made it easier for me. If they could handle it, so could I. Clinging to that thought, I always made it through my frequent bouts without uncontrollable nausea, but there were many times I wished I had joined the Army.

The next day the storm passed, and we fired up all four diesels in a futile effort to get into our designated position on time. We reached the Seishin Harbor area nearly a day past the shooting hour, with the element of surprise lost.

Weather conditions were slightly foggy, allowing us to get relatively near land before submerging. Despite the fog, conditions were good enough for our skipper to see smokestacks above the buildings, giving proof of an industrial city. Industry meant shipping, the ships would be there. Peering into the harbor from a safe distance through the periscope, the skipper saw no ships of consequence, only small fishing boats. But the main portion of the harbor was not visible, there had to be some worthwhile targets in there.

Moving away from that area, and the harbor's proximity, we surfaced to continue our hunt elsewhere. Eyes and radar probing the fog, we worked our way slowly along the coastline, hugging the shore to evaluate any activity worthy of photographing, or otherwise recording for our intelligence personnel. Also, there was the hope that we would come up on some cove anchorage with several ships just waiting to greet our torpedoes. We didn't stray too far from the Seishin area as we studied the coastline from a distance.

One thing visible on shore and of interest to our captain was a train with a long line of freight cars. The hour of the observation and the train's speed were noted. The captain had Birkner, the photographer, take pictures of it and the shoreline and beach: definite grounds for scuttlebutt about our future plans for that train. All speculation concerning these thoughts was put on hold though, we had another, more interesting attention-getter.

Weather conditions remained unchanged, and visibility for the lookouts remained limited. With radar working well and the Japanese cooperating, we picked up a distant target heading towards us. Hugging the coast, with the background making it difficult for enemy radar to pick us up, we waited and let the target close. By the time the ship came into view, we had her course and zigzag pattern well plotted.

Submerging and moving into an intercept course, we let the hapless vessel come to us. It was a medium-sized freighter, ripe for picking, completely oblivious to the imminent danger; but her zigzagging proved that her captain was aware of the possibility that an American stalker could be in the area. All of the Japanese captains had gotten the warning by now.

Our other submarines had made their presence known.

The skipper let her close course until he was satisfied with the distance and zig angle. The after room fired two torpedoes resulting in one hit. As the skipper watched the listing freighter slowly settling into the sea, some of its crew were abandoning ship, while the gun crews were firing at our periscope. To assure the sinking of the ship, another torpedo was fired. That torpedo was wasted; the ship sank as the torpedo approached. Score another for the *Flying Fish*. A morale lifter for our crew.

Leaving that scene of destruction, we followed a coastline course in the shipping lane between Seishin and Rashin. We would introduce ourselves to the Rashin Harbor area. With a little luck we could get some shooting before we reached Rashin.

Darkness set in and the foggy conditions increased, but the sea remained calm. The usual hunting pattern continued with lookouts straining their eyes and radar continuing its searching. For several hours, none of the war gods favored us. Then, radar, with its far reaching vision, picked up a target of respectable size. No other targets were visible on the screen. Obviously the ship was alone and its speed indicated that it was a merchant ship. On the surface, with our speed greater than that of the target, we continued on a steady overtake course while the target continued its zigzagging. With no escort to concern us, and the vessel not aware of our presence, we could choose our shooting position.

Below deck, we responded to the "Battle Stations Torpedo!" "Battle Stations Torpedo!" command and were standing by with excitement and anticipation. This was more like it should be. This was why we were here. Through Bennett on the battle phone, the order

118

came to make ready three tubes forward, followed by the command to open the tubes' outer doors. At our stations, we anxiously waited for the order to, "Fire," and it came.

Chapter 13

A Surface Torpedo Attack

Kawoof! "Number one fired!" The sound of the escaping torpedo and the shudder of the boat did not seem the same as that which I had previously experienced. This was the first surface torpedo firing since I had become a crew member. I was seated midway between the torpedo tubes, three on each side of me, my hands on the torpedo angle setting knobs. With a hand on each side of the dial, I turned the handles as quickly as I could, matching the commands from the TDC (torpedo data computer) which was located in the conning tower. My action was putting the commands directly into the torpedo guidance systems. Clang! Matt hit the firing valve with the palm of his hand. Again, the jarring sound and the shudder of the boat. Matt's voice, loud and clear, "Number two fired!"

The third was fired and we waited, counting the seconds, approximating the time of the explosions. The target was 1,100 yards away, traveling at a speed of 12 knots. The torpedo speed settings were at high, 45 knots. This gave us all that was needed for our calculation. The estimated time of contact was answered by an explosion. A hit! There was a brief period of cheering, mixed with comments of joy and bravado, none of compassion. We had just reduced, however slightly, the strength of America's foe. At that moment of success and conquest, there was little or no thought of the people who had been on the vessel.

Those on the top deck saw the flash of the explosion, dulled by the fog, approximately three seconds before hearing the sound. Slowly, and with utmost caution, we moved towards what radar showed to be a diminishing contact. Soon the radarman reported that the contact was disappearing. The sonarman reported breaking-up sounds. Apparently a secondary explosion within the vessel compounded the damage and contributed to the rapid sinking.

Matt, responsible for all that happened in the forward torpedo room, grumbled, "Old Man should have got that with one fish. Helluva waste of fish. We should get a lot more shooting. May run out of fish. What the hell will we do then, get ourselves killed trying to sink the bastards with our guns? Damn waste of fish." Matt was not willing to concede that Commander Risser's decision to fire three torpedoes was the correct one. We had no sighting of the ship and the torpedo firing was plotted entirely on radar bearings.

It was well past midnight, and we had been pursuing the lone vessel for nearly an hour through the very foggy night. Our radar, which initially detected the vessel, kept us in constant contact with the target. The vessel, a relatively small ship, either had no radar or its radar was faulty. It was obvious that those in command of the ship had word of the American submarines in their sea. They were steering an erratic course, wary, but unaware of our presence. The vessel continued in the same uncomplicated zigzag pattern. Undetected, we followed the unlighted ship, analyzed her zigzag pattern, and the spread of three torpedoes assured us a hit. She was ours!

The sinking of the ship near Seishin Harbor on the previous day was more or less accepted as just that. We sank an enemy ship. We gained a small victory. Little thought was given to the loss of lives directly attributed to the sinking. We simply did what was expected of us. We did it well and celebrated the victory. That sinking, a brief segment of the war, was in the past. We sank a ship from a distance, then turned away from the wreckage without close visual contact with anyone who had been on her. Not this sinking! From this night on, this portion of the war would be burned into our hearts and minds.

Very carefully, we approached what radar showed to be the remains of the vessel. Cries of pain and fear came from the foggy darkness. Cries of despair and hopelessness. Cries of men fighting for survival, clinging to bits of wreckage, fighting impossible odds. An eerie, gripping feeling came over all who heard those futile sounds. Muffled by the fog, they had a ghostly quality as they floated over the water's surface. Those on deck suffered those sounds. They could not turn away. We had a job to do.

It was not characteristic for a submarine to dally near its vanquished foe. We could not be absolutely certain that no message was transmitted from her before she sank, although our radioman did not have any evidence that any attempt was made to send one. Also, remaining in the same area, on the surface for such a long period of time, would be inviting near-certain destruction if an enemy submarine happened to come upon us undetected.

Our action was purposeful. Included in our orders was a mandate to take prisoners, and procure any documents which could be salvaged from a ship's wreckage. This sinking provided a fairly safe opportunity for that purpose. We were a long distance from the nearest land. With the night attack and early morning fog, circumstances could not have been better.

If an invasion of Japan became a reality, any information our intelligence people could extract from prisoners or gain from ships' charts would perhaps save American lives or otherwise be useful. We wanted to rescue two survivors. We were not bent on a rescue mission as such. We did not want any more than two of the enemy on our ship. We were early in our war patrol, with nearly two weeks in these waters remaining. Prisoners would be a great burden, and could interfere dangerously with the rapid and coordinated movement usually required in operation of a submarine. Our tight quarters would greatly compound the problem. This would be especially noticeable during battle stations or during a depth charge attack. The skipper thought that each torpedo room could deal with one prisoner comfortably.

Very slowly we maneuvered around and through the debris, guided more by the moans, cries and occasional communication of the unfortunate than anything else. With the passage of time, the voices became weaker and fewer. Injury and the very cold water were taking their toll. As dawn began to break, the wreckage and human forms became visible.

It was a sight which none who were on the *Flying Fish* deck will forget. It was one thing to destroy a ship, then undergo some depth charge retaliation while other enemy vessels rescued their ill-fated comrades. Somehow it was possible to divorce oneself from that act, as if the responsibility could be placed on the torpedoes or our captain. This was an entirely different set of circumstances. Here we had exposed the very heart of the war devil for all of us to see. I manipulated my feelings with arguments of justification. If I had known at the time that most of the victims were soldiers, it would have helped. It seemed to help later.

Then another disturbing thought pressed itself upon me. Suppose this had been a ship carrying factory workers? It could have been carrying factory workers and their families to a new location of work. Anything seemed possible in this hitherto protected and private sea.

Warriors we were, but even the most seasoned and most hardened on our boat were not celebrating the moment. But this was war; we too were being hunted. The purpose of our entry into the Sea of Japan was clear. We could not demoralize a nation without demonstrated destruction. The greater the destruction, the more effective it would be.

When there was enough light for safety and rescue action, we stopped amidst the wreckage. Commander Risser, using a Japanese language interpretation book, was making every effort to communicate with the poor souls who, for the most part, were hanging onto bits of wreckage too small to serve as temporary rafts. We doubted that our captain's struggle with the Japanese language was effective, but his intent must have been. Several men raised their heads, looked us over, and turned away. One man, dressed in a soldier's uniform, showed a desire to be rescued. Later we learned that he was one of the soldiers manning the ship's chief gun.

With our ballast tanks partially flooded so that our deck was nearly awash, we moved next to the intended prisoner. With help from two crew members, he was brought on board. The skipper made no attempt to rescue others, or take them by force. He must have been happy to quit there. We had been at the same spot for too long a time. And how would he have felt if eight or more had shown a desire to come aboard? Also, he undoubtedly wanted to put the appalling sight behind us as quickly as possible.

Before leaving to continue our hunting, en route to Rashin, we salvaged some floating documents. These documents gave general information about the ship but contained no important information. The ship was a freighter, 70 meters (230 feet) in length. Tonnage and other facts of no significant value were part of the printed material.

We left the staring eyes and flotsam with deep and weighty feelings. The sounds floating over the water grew weaker and no longer had any distinguishable human qualities. There was no doubt in the mind of anyone on the *Flying Fish* that those still alive were doomed.

Upper Left:
Cmdr. Robert D. Risser, seated alone. I regret I cannot identify the other officers.

Lower Left:
Cassel Evans cutting Joseph Kocon's hair.

Below:
Photographer Francis Birkner

Chapter 14

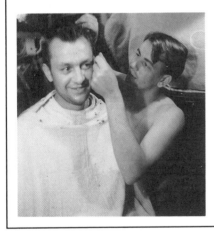

The Prisoner

"Hey! Look at the son-of-a-bitch, he's blue. First time I ever saw a blue Jap. Isn't he blue? Did you ever see a blue Jap before? Son-of-a-bitch is nearly froze. He's not even shivering. Must be too cold to shiver, nearly froze stiff." Stretch stood by closely scrutinizing the newest man on board.

The prisoner, whose clothing had been removed immediately after he was brought on the deck, sat naked on the makeshift barbering chair. Our first concern, at this point, was to protect ourselves against infestation of head or body lice. Evans, who was charged with the immediate responsibility for the prisoner, was also our ship's unofficial barber. He had finished up removing the hair from the prisoner's head, and motioned the prisoner to rise. He bounced the chair on its side, causing loose hair to fall to the floor-protecting mattress cover on which the Japanese now stood. With a smooth movement of his foot, he pushed the chair to the end of the mattress cover.

Looking at the sparse pubic hair, Evans placed the clippers on the chair, and picked up a safety razor from the end of the mattress cover. The prisoner, standing in the center of the mattress cover, seemed to show less concern. As Evans bent towards his intended task, presumed realization came upon the prisoner. He began to gyrate his lower body rapidly. Stretch howled with laughter, then paused. "Son-of-a-bitch knows you aren't a real barber. If you were a real barber, you'd be using a straight razor. Man, looks like he's practicing the hula. Wonder what he'd do if you broke out a straight razor? Anybody got a straight razor?"

Evans, forced into a task he did not relish one bit, began to show frustration with the prisoner and anger at Stretch. Matt, who along with all in the room was enjoying Stretch's monologue and Evans' discomfort, saw the need for intervention. "Knock it off, Stretch."

Stretch couldn't restrain himself from making one more remark, "Geez, he's blue. Are his balls blue too, Evans?" This brought another roar of laughter from everyone except Evans and the prisoner.

The gyrating hip movement was halted by the simple thrust of a service .45 into his midriff. Eyes closed, the prisoner stood rigid, accepting whatever fate was to befall him. The job finished, Evans stood up just as Doc, our Chief Pharmacist Mate, came in to make a visual inspection for head and body lice. Doc, Bill Whitefield, the only medic we had on the ship, was experienced and excellent in that capacity. He was also a caring and compassionate person who, after serving on surface vessels, had requested submarine duty. This was his second war patrol, and it was obvious that he had a special feeling for the *Flying Fish*. He was respected by all on the ship, for his personality as well as for his medical skill. Just days before, with extensive stitching, some bone setting and splinting, he undoubtly saved several fingers on the hand of a young cook's helper. The fingers had been severely damaged when a storage hatch fell on them.

Doc brought dungarees, a shirt and a cup of hot soup for the prisoner. When offered the cup, the prisoner shunned it until Evans took a swallow, then he readily accepted the soup.

Stretch couldn't resist, he had one more comment. "Don't know why 'Tojo' was so worried, can't do much with that little thing anyway." The name "Tojo," a reference to Japan's general and statesman who directed the attack against Pearl Harbor, stuck. Stretch beat Matt to that one.

The comments by Stretch, and our reaction to them, may have been a means of compensating for the feelings and thoughts which affected us so strongly a short while before as we witnessed, closeup, the destruction our torpedo attack had caused. Also, there is a certain toughness expected of warriors. It was almost as if there had to be a less compassionate feeling for the prisoner. He was not one of the unfortunate ones left behind.

For the first few days it was difficult to accept this enemy's presence. We did not brutalize him in any physical way, but we did demonstrate our dislike for him. When he did not move rapidly enough to satisfy us, he was urged on by threatening movements towards the service .45. Once, Evans took a diver's knife, pantomimed hari-kari and extended the knife, handle first, to him. Tojo backed away, a very concerned look on his face. When one of us who had room watch felt a little bored or perhaps a little mean, we would wake Tojo and put him to work at some minor clean-up task. Little regard was given to how long he had been awake or how much he had been worked during the previous watch.

Each of us had private thoughts related to the prisoner. I was troubled by the comfortable condition he had and would continue to have after he was turned over to authorities when our patrol run ended, as compared to the Americans whom the Japanese held as prisoners. The fact that one of my hometown friends was one of those held prisoner accentuated my feelings. Rescued American prisoners of war gave firsthand proof that most of them had received harsh treatment from their Japanese captors.

Two days after we took Tojo into the forward torpedo room, we made a bet with the after torpedo room crew. The bet was that by the time we reached home port, our torpedo tubes would be cleaner and brighter than those in the after room. There were six tubes forward and four aft. Crew member numbers gave the after room a proportional advantage.

The torpedo tubes were made of bronze. The cylindrical body had an orange-peel texture. The doors were smoothly finished. The tubes in either room had never been polished. At best, they were given a general wipe-down to remove excess grease or an accumulation of oxide caused by the salt water and air exposure. They appeared more greenish than bronze colored.

Members of the two rooms didn't exchange visits often. There was seldom any time for periods of casual visits. It was several days before word of our trickery was out. The crew of the after room didn't consider the help we would get from Tojo. There was much complaining until we offered this solution: "Okay, it will be Tojo against the entire after room crew. All of you combined should be able to out-do one little Jap." That ended the complaints, either because they had planned to honor the bet as it was originally anyway, or because the thought of us cracking the whip on Tojo appealed to them.

Tojo was an intelligent and pragmatic person who must have quickly evaluated his present state and came to the conclusion that, under the circumstances, he wasn't all that bad off. He tried to please in all things we expected of him. I had the watch when Tojo, using a wire brush on a hard-to-get-at place, broke a grease fitting off number four tube. Obviously concerned, he motioned me over and pointed to the broken fitting. With another motion he indicated that the part which broke off was down in the bilges. I had some understanding of his concerns. He had no way of knowing how serious the damage was or how his young guard would react to it. His honesty touched me and with a look of compassion I assured him that I was not angry. Then I handed the scouring powder to him and pointed to the torpedo tube doors.

As the reader must suspect, by the time we reached our first home port on Midway Island, our tubes were sparkling. There was no doubt about which room won the bet. A young officer was selected as the judge. He was amazed at the beauty of the tubes. I suppose the after room crew knew from the beginning what the outcome would be. Some of them even complimented us on the great work we got out of Tojo.

In just a few days after having Tojo with us, we began to accept him as a suffering human being. Although we were still firm and continued to point him towards the torpedo tubes and his assigned task, we sat with him and established some degree of communication. Motions plus pencil and paper were the best means for making ourselves understood. We soon learned that Tojo would tell us only what he chose to tell. He communicated freely about his family. He was 34 years old. He had a wife and four children, two of each sex. We didn't learn that he was with the Philippine invasion force until the expert interrogators at Midway got that out of him.

Tojo didn't create any special problems during the remainder of the patrol. If anything, he helped break the monotony during the slow hours. He was a nuisance in a small way. His pallet was on the floor, where he was kept shackled to the end of a torpedo tube rack. He became an obstruction in our tight quarters when he was not free and working at his assigned task. Most ships of larger size had a brig for problem people.

At his request, we provided him with pencil and paper. We thought he was writing a letter to his family. Much of his free time was devoted to the writing. He always had the same serious expression when he wrote, no other emotion showed through. The Japanese characters were neat and interesting but meaningless to us. He kept the paper and pencil wrapped in a clean wipe-rag and stowed it under his pallet when he was not writing. As time went by, Tojo grew more relaxed. He no longer looked at us for signs of disapproval when he reached to retrieve or return his writing material.

He ate his food from a bowl and used the provided spoon. The food was the same as that which we ate and the portions were equal. He seemed to relish our food and ate with gusto. We joked about conditions being so comfortable for him that we would be forced to drag him off our boat when we reached port.

After the war's end, Tojo, just as many other warriors on both sides of the conflict, would continue to fight the demons within. He no doubt would have some sense of guilt stemming from his good fortune in being alive. Other unpleasant war experiences he may have had would simply compound his war with the demons. But even today, I take solace from the fact that our effort did return one lucky warrior to his family and friends.

This torpedo is on display at the Maritime Museum, Astoria, Oregon.

Dimensions: Length — 20 feet
Diameter — 21 inches

Chapter *15*

Hot, Straight and Normal

Late morning of June 12, we reached the Rashin Harbor entrance. Visibility was about 500 yards and we remained on the surface, slowly closing the distance to the harbor. Radar indicated a small vessel, which we thought to be a patrol boat, leaving the harbor at a distance of 4,000 yards. We submerged and the vessel passed us at about half that distance. With the patrol vessel searching the more distant waters, we moved into the harbor's entrance. The fog was not cooperating and the moorage sites were not visible. The fog was both foe and friend. As Matt put it, "If the fog should lift suddenly, we'll be sitting ducks. Who knows what's in that harbor? The water's too damn shallow to dive. All we could do is shoot and run."

Later sightings and screw-sound recognition told us that the vessel previously sighted was indeed a patrol vessel. In a way it was amusing to us, the guard dog off chasing shadows while the predator was snuggling up to the flock.

We remained offshore and in the general area of the harbor entrance for several hours, noting a patrol plane scouting almost constantly. Once, as the plane approached, we made the usual precautionary dive.

While we were submerged, the fog lifted and through the periscope two small freighters were sighted. Without the fog and with the presence of the plane, we made a submerged run in an attempt to get within shooting range. No such luck. The vessels continued in the direction of Seishin, unaware of our presence.

The following day, on the surface and still in the harbor vicinity, we sighted two other freighters. One was large and the other of medium size. Two escorts accompanied the freighters. One of the escorts was the cooperative patrol boat; the other, a modified trawler. We would make a submerged attack.

Ah-oo-gah! Ah-oo-gah! These blasts from the Klaxon and the *Flying Fish* nosed downward, seeking obscurity and the relative safety of the deep water. We submerged sooner than we would have liked to, but conditions seemed to demand this action. The skipper had to make a decision whether to remain on the surface and, with the advantage of surface speed, move into a better shooting position, or dive and settle for what he could get with the set-up he had. Remaining on the surface to close the distance would be chancing both detection and being bombed. It would heighten the possibility of no shooting and the certainty of a depth charge pounding as our near-exact location became known to the enemy.

Gently and smoothly, our boat slipped into the water and was leveled off at ninety feet. Water was forced from or added to various ballast tanks which surrounded her hull. This was done to get a balance fore and aft and to attain neutral buoyancy throughout the length of the ship. This accomplished, the bow and stern operators, on orders from the diving officer, brought the ship to periscope depth.

In her proper element, the hidden depths, the

Flying Fish became the silent, fearsome, deadly, and efficient destroyer of enemy ships she was designed to be. This was her sole purpose for being, and this was the intent of the men whom she housed. Information gained through periscope observations had to be coordinated. The target distance, speed, direction of travel, angle on the bow, and time for torpedo intercept courses all had to mesh. The tracking party and the plot team would put all the information together as a well-trained and practiced team.

There was a tension within the *Flying Fish* which permeated her entire length. Would we be able to get into shooting position? The approach to Rashin Harbor was near, but still far from the targets' intended moorage. We would make every attempt to give them a permanent resting place before they reached the harbor.

Our surface sinking of the prisoner's ship three nights ago was not forgotten. It was fresh in our minds, but there was also the totally encompassing realization that the war had to end quickly and with the American side victorious. We had to do our part, and the present circumstances demanded that we concentrate on the immediate situation confronting us. All other thoughts did not need to be pushed aside, they were automatically displaced for the time being by minds trained to respond to the instantaneous demands of war.

Soon after the plotting team was ordered to the control room, Evans undid the prisoner's leg-iron from the torpedo rack. When the passageway was clear of traffic he took him to the dining room. There, our prisoner's leg-iron was secured to a fixed table leg. He would be left alone, alone to suffer through what would be a frightening experience for any un-initiated human.

We waited. We were ready. Everything was in order in the forward torpedo room and we were all eager for the kill, but there was another thought weighing on our minds. Our uncontested sinking of a lone, unsuspecting vessel was unusual, a vessel completely at our mercy with no escort vessels to protect her or to retaliate with the usual depth charge attack. Even the few crew members making their first patrol run knew the danger and probability of a depth charge retaliation following the firing on escorted vessels.

We accepted what seemed like the inevitable. We had confidence in our skipper's ability to elude the enemy. That confidence extended to every man serving on the *Flying Fish*. We would rise to the demands of any occasion. And if we could not quickly shake the enemy, the *Flying Fish* would not let us down. She had proven many times that she was a tough old girl. We had a boat capable of withstanding any explosion which wasn't nearly on target. But there was a new concern. Intelligence sources learned that the Japanese were now using 600-pound depth charges. Previously they had used 350-pound charges. The heavier charges could mean a death-dealing blow from an explosion 30 feet away, as compared to 20, the estimated distance required for a 350-pound depth charge to hole a hull. Our evasive skills were good, and our boat was sound with no worn parts making telltale sounds. Still, how good or lucky would the enemy be? How near would the depth charges explode?

The battle stations alarm sounded. The rapid "gong! gong! gong! gong!" triggered an instant rush of adrenaline. "Battle stations torpedo! Battle stations

torpedo! Battle stations torpedo!" A seemingly unnecessary command, but it, along with the continuous gonging, stimulated another response from the
adrenaline glands.

We waited. Soon word came from the conning
tower commanding, "Make ready all torpedo tubes
forward and aft. Open all outer doors. Reloading
crews stand by." Matt and Canaday turned the
wrenches, opening the outer torpedo tube doors.
Beginning with one and two, the two top tubes, they
worked their way down with every possible speed. The
effort brought perspiration to Matt's brow. Canaday's
only sign of exertion was his increased breathing.

Bennett was on the battle phones, standing near
the bulkhead, away from the tube doors. I was in my
position on the walkway, facing forward, between the
torpedo tubes, manning the torpedo data computer
(TDC) relay. I was prepared to crank the commands
which came from the conning tower, directly into the
torpedo guidance systems.

Stretch, standing ready as part of the reload crew,
said, "Geez, what do we have up there, the whole Jap
Navy?"

Matt, in between grunts and turns said, "Knock
it off, Stretch!" It was always a race to see if we could
beat the after room whenever all tubes were made
ready. From Matt, "Outer doors open forward, tubes
ready for firing."

After relaying Matt's report Bennett grimaced,
"They beat us."

With the boat at 65 feet, the skipper lowered the
observation periscope and raised the more slender
attack periscope. At that depth, waves washed over it
occasionally. To have it extended higher above the
water's surface would be inviting detection. To fur-

ther reduce that possibility, he was making quick observations, intermittently raising and lowering the periscope. The readings he gave on the bearing, range and bow angle of each target, plus the speed, when properly introduced into the torpedo data computer, (although crude by today's standards) would be quickly assimilated in its electronic brain and provide the shooting solution. If the information was correct and the target proceeded as predicted, all would go well for us. The assumption was that the torpedoes would function properly. They did not always do so.

In our submerged state, there was no possibility of decreasing the range or in any other way improving our shooting position. The skipper had to take what was given. The shooting would have to be done quickly and accurately.

Bennett, our telephone contact with the conning tower, kept us informed in his quiet but resonant voice, "We have two targets and two escorts up there. The range is long and the angle is tough. It's going to take some good shooting." His voice changed to one of loud, crisp command, "Stand by one!" All through this period of time, I was busy on the TDC relay. "Fire one!"

Matt hit the firing valve with the heel of his hand. "Number one fired!" The boat shuddered as air pressure forced the 2,800-pound torpedo towards the open sea.

The forward movement of the torpedo caused its starting lever to trip, immediately forcing alcohol under pressure into a combustion pot. A series of relatively simple but ingenious devices caused a series of chain reactions. Water forced into the combustion pot, just beyond the burning alcohol, was converted into steam. Air, compressed to 3,000 lbs. per sq. inch and stored in a compartment making up about one fourth of the torpedo's length, was released to force the high pressure steam over two drive-turbines connected directly to the propeller shafts. The rapid turning of the torpedo's propellers would give them control over propulsion even before the torpedo completely cleared the tube.

Matt reached up and opened a vent valve, called a poppet valve. The poppet valve opened into the bilges and allowed the air, which had started the forward motion of the torpedo, to accept the area of least resistance and be forced back into the boat by the sea water, even before the tapered tail of the torpedo had left the tube. To allow the huge air bubble to escape into the sea would be like sending a beacon to the enemy. The torpedo tube almost instantly filling, the sea water began to hiss in the bilges, creating a cloud of fog around the lower tubes.

Matt closed the poppet valve. The sea water within the tube would help compensate for the torpedo weight loss and maintain the boat's equilibrium. Tubes two and three were fired, and treated the same way. The firing was at eight-second intervals, a tight spread. There was a brief interlude while the shooting bearings were finalized on the second target. The command came. Torpedoes four, five and six were fired.

Without waiting for orders, Matt began preparing for reloading. He and Canaday closed the outer doors. Next, they opened the drain valves which connected the tubes to a special holding tank. Through another system, air under pressure was released into the tubes, forcing water from the tubes and into the holding tank. When the tube was free of water and the pressure was equal to that in the boat, it was possible to open the inner tube door safely.

The targets, drawing considerable water, indicated that they carried heavy loads. They were 1900 yards away. To this country boy, that represented a "stretched" mile. The course of the targets would continue to slightly increase the distance. About one and one-half minutes would be required for our torpedo run. Our boat was brought around, positioning for a stern-tube attack. Big ships can take a lot of sinking, especially if they're not hit midships. Bennett quietly announced, "Sonar reports torpedoes running hot, straight and normal." Music to our ears. We and the ordnance people had done our job well.

Then shooting conditions deteriorated so none of the stern tubes were fired.

With high hopes we counted off the time required for the expected explosions. The time expired without any explosion. Bennett's voice, "We're going deep, escort headed our way!" The bow tilted sharply and the order to rig for depth charge attack was given. At about the same time we heard distant explosions, as the torpedoes hit the beach. Obvious misses! What happened? Did a plane spot us and warn them? Did the skipper make a slight error? Did the plotting team screw up? Did they spot the torpedo wakes? Did the escort pick up the sound of the torpedoes early in their run? The last was least likely since the escort was moving too rapidly for that type of surveillance. Most likely we had been spotted by a plane and the ships were warned. Perhaps it was the same scout plane which was working the area earlier.

This was not the time to contemplate any of that. The escort, bristling with guns and loaded depth charge racks, was bearing down on us. We went down deep and rigged for silent running. We would hide from the enemy, with the *Flying Fish* at 250 feet, hydraulic systems shut down and most of the most basic functions in manual operation. No one had to be reminded how well sound travels through water and every precaution was taken to reduce noise.

The enemy was deliberate in their electronic search but the pinging was some distance away. They must have picked up something in that area and mistook it for us. Several depth charges were dropped, but none near us. Our exact location was not known to them. The first escort was joined by her companion and they continued to search for us, never getting very near.

We continued in silent running until all contact with the escorts was lost. After a quick periscope look, we secured from silent running. Matt cleared with the diving officer for tube reloading. There was no big hurry, by now the ships were safely in the harbor.

The racks which held the reload torpedoes were on tracks. The rack was forced into a position where the torpedo was in line with the torpedo tube, and the rack was locked into that position. A block and tackle arrangement, similar to that used in a factory or on a farm, was used to force the torpedo into the tube. If the boat was steady, we never used the block and tackle for the last two feet. (Matt and I used the same method we employed during the dry dock fire in Pearl Harbor.) In doing this, we accelerated and simplified the loading process. This could not have been done safely if the boat was not held steady. It was the responsibility of the diving officer to make things as safe and easy as possible for the loading crew.

With the reload complete, the forward room crew drank coffee and relaxed, but not for long. On the surface, and moving slowly inland, another freighter came into sight.

This, a medium sized vessel, was not escorted and we made a hard run to get into firing position. Her crew experienced the scare of their lives, but the ship eluded us by making the entrance to a small harbor well ahead of torpedo range.

Depth charge or bomb explosions sounded at a distance. Communication from the freighter must have alerted the patrol boats, and they were doing what they could from a distance to scare us off. We dove when a plane approached. Soon after, the patrol boat, accompanied by four trawlers modified to carry depth charge racks, searched our immediate area without detecting us. As soon as they gave up, we surfaced again.

The air was heavy with disappointment as we tried to restore a normal routine. Evans brought Tojo back. He appeared frightened and had a hangdog appearance. We couldn't resist making depth charge and torpedo exploding motions to him. Perhaps that was our way of venting our frustration. Tojo had no way of knowing that our attack was fruitless. To him, the torpedoes exploding on the beach indicated a sinking.

I visited the after torpedo room and exchanged thoughts with Pete. The solemn air persisted in the forward room and through the boat. A rare opportunity was lost. Big freighters were getting to be a scarce item and six expensive torpedoes were wasted. The ships which remained out of shooting range deepened our disappointment.

We had stirred the waters in this area enough for now. Better to let things settle down, then we would try the Rashin Harbor area again in a few days. We steered a course south for Seishin. We buoyed our spirits with statements such as, "Better hunting elsewhere. The Sea of Japan will provide!"

Top — With Warren F. Wildes, Electrician Third Class, and Ralph C. Beardsley, Signalman First Class, standing behind the 40-mm gun, Harold Holloway and the author are in firing position. Bottom — The author in the forward torpedo room.

Chapter 16

Battle Stations, Guns

Occasional, distant plane pips on radar kept us alert as we moved seaward and headed southwest towards Seishin, away from the area of missed opportunity and frequent plane activity. Bennett, in his quiet but clear voice said, "Well gang, I don't think any of us can label today as a boring day. How about it, Matt, what can you compare it to?"

Matt snorted, "Total disappointment! Too damn bad we couldn't have gotten into better shooting position. Just a lot of bad luck for us. Call it a lucky day for the Japs."

After an uneventful night, we moved in near the shoreline under dense fog. Our radar showed a number of small targets between us and shore. Through the fog, the first to come into view were three sail-topped cargo vessels.

We approached the lead boat and our captain, using his American-Japanese translation book, urged the people to abandon their vessel. That brought no results. Then, 50-caliber rounds were fired into the hull. That action resulted in a scamper for the cabin. On orders, Pete and I put several 40-mm rounds into the bow of one vessel. That did the job and the crew pushed off in a small boat. We commenced firing into the boat's hull. The vessel was loaded with lumber and despite a large hole the 40-mm explosions made at her water line, she didn't even list. The *Flying Fish* was brought about so that the five-inch gun could be put into action. One round from the five-inch and she broke in the center. With lumber sliding to the slanted and broken middle, she was finished.

We pursued the other two boats, which were slightly larger than the one we had just destroyed. With 40-mm fire we brought the mast down on one of them, leaving it dead in the water. Once again our boat was brought about so that the five-inch could go to work. With the one vessel disabled, the five-inch gunners gave their attention to the one under way. Several rounds from that gun demolished it.

While this was happening, the fog lifted slightly and two tugs came into view. One of them was towing a string of ten small barges, the other towed two. Their intent was to crowd the shore and their course was almost directly shoreward. The gunfire had alerted them. With the barges in tow, their progress was slow. We turned the 40-mm on the string of ten, firing 40-mm rounds into the barges. We had closed to within 200 yards of the end barge — not a very long golf ball flight — and comfortable shooting distance for a deer hunter. Taking them as Sergeant York took his turkeys - shooting the last in line first, we began working our way up the string of barges with 40-mm fire. The barges were loaded with bricks, and particles of shattered bricks reached the deck of the *Flying Fish*.

As our 40-mm rounds knocked the sterns out of the barges, the sterns sank and the bricks spilled out as they would from a dump truck. With the sterns under water, the wooden vessels still had enough buoyancy for the forward movement of the tug to keep a portion of the bow above water. After sinking most of them, and with the tug still slowly making its way to shore, the captain commanded, "Get the tug! Get the tug!" I looked up at him. He didn't have a look of exuberance in his eyes. It was apparent that this action was as unpleasant for him as it was for us. He had his orders — "Shoot everything, sink everything, create as much havoc as possible and strike fear into the hearts of the people with whose nation we were at war!"

I asked Pete, an arm's length away, "Do we want to kill those poor bastards?" Pete didn't answer.

The captain's command, now louder and firmer, "Dammit, get that tug!" ended any deliberation. As we turned our fire on the tug, the two-man-crew came out of the cabin. One scrambled over the bow, the other fell to the deck. The tug's stern settled on the bottom in shallow water while the fortunate crew member seemed to be flying over waist-deep water as he made his way to shore.

As Pete and I were working the barges over, the five-inch gunners finished off the other tug and the vessel previously disabled, with its mast and sail partially in the water but mainly on the deck.

With no other targets visible and the radar screen giving no indication of any at a distance, the damaged tug was on line for total destruction, but circumstances prevented that. The *Flying Fish* could not be brought about to bring the five-inch gun to bear on it. Our boat had very little water under her keel; so little that the depth gauge did not register. We did an "all back full" and gained adequate water for maneuverability.

The fog continued to lift and the sky showed patches of clearing. This was not the time or place to greet an enemy plane. Shallow water and no chance to dive would leave us vulnerable. But, since we were manning the guns and ready, with a little luck Pete and I might have blasted a plane or two out of the sky before the situation became deadly serious. The 40-mm was considered a key anti-aircraft gun, and during our training, we forced the controllers of the drone target to put it beyond range on several occasions. We gained deep water, secured from battle stations and proceeded in the direction of Seishin Harbor.

Below deck, reaction was muted. None of us took pride in the minuscule dent we may have put in Japan's war supplies. In the forward room, we discussed the incident quietly. Reminding each other of the patrol's true purpose, we justified our action and eased our minds. But it seemed that from that day, we showed more compassion for our prisoner.

Putting the minor destruction behind us, we headed for Seishin. From the previous observations, that harbor appeared to have much shipping activity.

Chapter 17

Dashed Promises

The fog began to lift as we neared Seishin. We dived and proceeded towards the harbor entrance. Commander Risser decided to move to the harbor entrance for close reconnaissance.

The following is from the declassified patrol report, just as it was printed.

June 15, 1945

1300-1500 - Closed in to 2400 yards from breakwater at Seishin. Observed three loaded AK's, one light AK, and possibly one other at dock inside breakwater: no chance for torpedo fire. Took pictures, watched trains pulling in and out, etc. Much small traffic: Launches, fishing boats, tugs, barges, etc. Had a few anxious moments when one small tug with two barges in tow got pretty close. I dropped down to 90 feet and went ahead two thirds to clear him. He was passing down port side very close when his screws suddenly stopped. Came up to look and one of the barge steersmen could have spit on the periscope.

He didn't see us but my quick look showed the barges full of large boulders. A new breakwater is apparently being built close in or else the other one is being extended. I had visions of the Flying Fish forming part of it. We stood out, saw more tugs with rock laden barges standing down from the north. Also sighted, standing in, a small trawler apparently belonging to the coast guard. He had two mast fully as high as he was long, with crow's nests on each. He was towing a small tug — Probably one of those we damaged this morning.

1901 - Surfaced and stood seaward. Visibility poor.

Further patrolling in the area produced nothing worth torpedo expenditure, so we worked our way seaward, towards the shipping lanes. We had not had any fighting action for four days. Soon after leaving the harbor area, radar sighted two vessels. Before we could get into position they made the harbor entrance.

June 20, 1945

0324 - Commenced closing KOMATSUSAN TAN to investigate seaward suburb of Seishin.

0434 - Visibility very poor. Commenced surface patrol about 9000 yards off beach

0942 - Visibility increasing rapidly. Dived and headed in.

1200 - Nothing in this vicinity but the usual small tugs with barges. We have better plans for our five-inch gun. Commenced rounding point and entering Seishin Harbor.

1530 - We are getting close now. Plan to look over the situation and make battle surface on moored ships about sunset.

1542 - Commenced raining.

1550 - JP sound contact on heavy screws at 085 degrees R.

1601 - Sighted a standard (modified) cargo ship standing into port range at 2500 yards. Swung right.

1607 - Fired first of a salvo of three torpedoes forward, average gyro angle 350 degree, run 1250, track 120 degrees P. This was a fast set up but very good. Used ST ranges and periscope bearings. Couldn't miss angle on the bow, it was so near 90 degrees. Speed was not well known of course but bearing continued to check right on with that generated for some time after firing. Torpedoes ran hot and straight by sound.

1611 - First of three torpedoes hit the beach. Target turned just three minutes after firing but this was probably a normal course change to enter port.

1710 - Echo ranging from direction of inner harbor. Heard screws very shortly afterwards. Visibility very poor now.

1717 - ST contact 1600 yards on pinger — a little too late for surfacing and running now. Commenced increasing depth.

1721 - First of thirteen depth charges — not close but dropped very deliberately — all astern.

1729 - Another set of screws on opposite quarter from pinger.

1739 - Lost contact on 1729 ship.

1811 - Echo ranging very weak — at periscope depth. Pinger still not sighted but had possible pip on ST at 6150 yards.

1830 - All clear on the sound and ST.

1845 - Surfaced and stood seaward to patrol off coast.

After surfacing, we played radar cat and mouse with the patrol boat for nearly an hour before eluding it. We then made way for the vicinity of the harbor again. No pickings there, so the next day we started working our way back to Rashin. Our extensive and formally promising hunting didn't even turn up gun fodder.

There was a time during this "dry" period when Matt approached me with a suggestion that we go ashore and lay explosives under the track to destroy the train. I agreed to what may or may not have been a seriously-planned opportunity to strike that blow against the enemy. The idea had been discussed by the captain and other officers, but the degree of commitment was questionable. I never pressed Matt for details of the proposed caper.

On June 23, we made a run at a ship which turned

out to be a Russian vessel. Later that same day we sighted another ship, a big one. We dived with high hopes, but it was also a Russian vessel.

The remainder of our patrolling was uneventful, and on June 24, we headed for our rendezvous point in preparation for exiting the Sea of Japan.

Chapter 18

Bless the Fog, Damn the Enemy

Wearing dark glasses, and under red lights for better eye adaptation to night vision, the *Flying Fish* gun crews stood crowded in the dining room and in the control room. We, the men who would man the guns, with our support teams, the ammunition handlers and loader.

Except for a small ready locker on deck, all of the ammunition was stored beneath the dining room, and had to be passed by human chain up through the hatches. With our one five-inch gun, one 40-millimeter gun and two 20-millimeter guns, we didn't have much firepower compared to most surface fighting vessels, but we were ready for the battle stations command. We would do with what we had, hoping for the best and prepared for the worst.

After 16 days in the Sea of Japan, on a scheduled midnight hour, eight submarines rendezvoused just inside the La Perouse Strait. The date was June 24, 1945. The submarines were the *Bowfin, Crevalle, Flying Fish, Sea Dog, Skate, Spadefish, Tinosa,* and the *Tunny.* The *Bonefish,* our ninth submarine, was not among us. There was some brief communication between boats and a summary of the ships sunk was exchanged. One of the skippers, who had the patrol area adjacent to that of the *Bonefish*, reported hearing heavy and sustained depth charge explosions from her patrol vicinity several days earlier. We waited an additional 24 hours hoping for some communication from the *Bonefish*. Under the circumstances, this was a dangerous thing to do. Stealth offered our best chance for a safe exit from the Sea of Japan. Eight submarines in a relatively small area were risking detection. After our 24-hour vigilant wait, we accepted what seemed obvious and acted on our plans to depart Hirohito's private bathtub, leaving the *Bonefish* behind.

Pete and I shook hands. It wasn't an actual handshake, just one grip and a strong squeeze; an action of assurance and support. We did not speak. No one in the room spoke. This was a time for private thought and perhaps silent prayer. We waited as the cold fresh air funneled through the conning tower and control room hatches, sharpening our senses. There was no sign of fear or even concern, only evidence of determination and resolve.

Our four diesel engines, throbbing in unison, powered, us at a speed of 18 knots through the cold waters and the fog-laden air of the La Perouse Strait.

Naval Intelligence reports showed the strait to be mined at a depth which allowed passage of surface vessels but would make it virtually impossible to dive safely or to navigate through it as we did through the Tsushima Strait. The water was shallow as compared to that of the Tsushima Strait. Submerged exit was beyond consideration. Our apprehension was heightened by intelligence reports indicating that the Japanese had surveillance equipment at a narrow portion of the strait. As to whether there would be any vessels patrolling the area, we could only guess.

Exiting via our entry route was not practical, because strong currents moving with us would make accurate steering very difficult. Maneuvering through that or any minefield was precarious business. There was no better choice, this was to be our exit route.

There was a seemingly bright spot in all of this. If any of our boats were severely damaged but still under power, the neutral port of Vladivostok was a refuge if it could be reached. Several days ago, this had been a hot topic of discussion in the forward torpedo room, and we had concluded that it wouldn't be unpleasant duty for the remainder of the war, spending the time with a Russian lass in the area of Vladivostok. But in the face of reality, we realized the sanctuary would be a possibility only if attempted before we had progressed very far into the strait. A run for Vladivostok would require a near 180-degree course reversal and a great distance of hazardous travel through enemy-controlled water.

In an attempt to confuse the Japanese and direct their thinking and efforts towards the Tsushima Strait, an American submarine shelled an island in that strait on the night of our originally planned departure. Our forces had no way of knowing that we would be departing a day later than scheduled. That submarine did draw overt attention and avoided a depth charge attack by hasty retreat. The shelling intended to appear as a parting insult from one of our group as we were putting the Sea of Japan behind us.

Everyone on the boat knew that if we had to shoot our way out, it would be a win-or-die situation. There would be no diving to the comparative safety of deep water, and the neutral port of Vladivostok was considered more of a hope than a practicality. Most of us must have realized that even if gunfire did not get us, the icy water flowing from the Arctic would if we lost our boat. The Japanese would have a great desire to rescue survivors from whom they could possibly extract information. The rescue would in fact be a capture.

My personal thought was that death would be preferable to capture. After the way we submariners had ravaged their shipping lanes, not only these past weeks, but all through the war years, the anger we had actuated in the enemy would have no bounds. My belief was that the Japanese would probably invent methods of unique torture just for us. The very heavy toll of their warships and merchant vessels must have been a gnawing frustration. I was not seriously concerned about being captured. The foggy night, the icy water and the current would grant me my preference if the time should come.

Much would depend on the accuracy of every gun on each of the eight submarines. Individually, our firepower was wanting, but the combined guns and possible surface torpedo firings — if the opportunity became available — would make us a formidable force to deal with. I used the early minutes to steel my mind and resolved to ignore enemy fire. Pete and I would do our part; we were very accurate with the 40-millimeter gun.

Standing in the control room with only infrequent hushed voices imposing on my thoughts, my mind seemed in harmony with the smooth throbbing of the engines. I compared my responsibility to that of my shipmates and their duties below deck, if and when the shooting started.

Everyone on the boat would be at their assigned battle station, ready to respond instantly to any command or need. This would be the case on the bridge, in the conning tower and control room, as well as in the maneuvering room, engine rooms, and the forward and after torpedo rooms. The cooks, stewards, and others of the crew not assigned to some specific item of machinery would be in the ammunition passing line.

At this hour of seeming inevitability, given the choice, I wouldn't have traded places with any of them. In a way, their fate would be in our hands, the hands of us doing direct battle with the enemy. The gun crews and those passing ammunition up through the hatches wouldn't have time for thinking other thoughts. But what about the others standing by at their stations, confined to their respective compartments? They could do nothing except visualize the action above through the bits of information which came via the communication system or filtered down through the hatches. They would be listening to the gunfire and wishing the best for us. And too, they couldn't help but wonder about an enemy shell striking our hull near their compartment.

In two columns, spaced for maneuverability and attack, holding a steady course at three-quarter speed, with radar scanning and lookouts straining their eyes, we made our way through the strait. It has been said that the night is no man's friend. Every man on each of the eight submarines was in a position to disprove that statement.

With each mile we progressed, our passage became all the more perilous as we committed our vessel farther into the waters over the minefield and toward the unknown. There was concern that the Japanese had a destroyer base near the outlet of the strait. The destroyer — the greatest threat to the submarine — had it all: many guns, torpedoes, depth charges, excellent radar, great maneuverability, twice our speed, and men to spare. I tried to weigh our chances against several destroyers and quickly erased such thoughts from my mind, replacing them with fighting thoughts. I adopted a fatalistic attitude toward our circumstances and my thinking changed to, "Come on you bastards, we'll take you on!"

A very foggy night favored us. Early in our passage, we passed one vessel at a distance but were not challenged. It may have been a Russian ship. Or it may have been a Japanese vessel whose crew thought us to be a fleet of fishing boats returning from the fishing grounds. Time dragged on. Then, without any spoken word or explanation for it, the tension seemed to ease, almost as if the *Flying Fish* was telling us that the crux of our passage was behind us. Soon word came to secure from battle stations. After what seemed like an eternity, we were through the La Perouse Strait! Once again the enemy had been fooled.

In the semi-darkness Pete, and I grinned at each other. We both nodded but spoke no words. As I turned toward the forward torpedo room, he gave me a hearty slap on the back. Half turning, I gave him a mock salute and continued on my way.

We welcomed the Sea of Okhotsk with its unmined deep water as we erased doubts about a safe return to a home port. Soon we were skirting the Bering Sea and passing the Kuril Islands on a beautiful sunny morning. The water, with icebergs floating in it, was so placid that a rowboat would have been adequate as a means of transportation. The *Flying Fish* glided along as smoothly as her namesake would. These were the kinds of conditions which could lull weary warriors into a complacent sense of false security. The danger to us was greatly diminished, but it was still lurking and I felt that I had to remind myself of that fact.

Our nine submarines had done their job well, and were leaving behind much destruction. Resting on the bottom of the Sea of Japan, and scattered over large diversified areas of that sea, were a total of 28 Japanese ships and 16 small craft. Add to that, five ships and three small craft damaged. Every submarine had scored and left its mark!

How important was the effect of all of our destruction on the people of Japan? We left behind a more demoralized nation. Now, no part of that country could be considered safe from the forces of the United States, a fact, which, by the time of our exit from the Sea of Japan, must have been recognized by the Japanese even in the remote regions of that country. The sinking of so many vessels in so many different areas in a 16-day period had to be Japan's most talked-about topic since their sneak attack on Pearl Harbor. Until our penetration into the Sea of Japan, the Japanese thought those waters impenetrable to their enemy. What a shock it must have been to wake up one morning and learn that the major harbors bordering "their sea" were under siege. Our objective had been accomplished.

Pappy, still obviously troubled about our area of patrol, spoke to no specific person, "I wonder what good we did by shooting up those small Korean boats?"

Once again giving evidence of his varied and extensive reading, Canaday had the answer: "Pappy, I think it was General Sherman who said, 'War is cruel and the crueler it is, the quicker it will be over.' We did what was expected of us. Don't think for one minute that the Japs wouldn't be doing the same or worse to us if they had the chance."

Matt nodded agreement, "Remember what the bastards did at Pearl Harbor? And they didn't stop there; they killed civilians in Honolulu. Some of the planes on that Pearl Harbor attack were probably flown by Korean pilots. And those ships we sank, who do you think they were helping in the war effort?" Then, stabbing the air with a finger directed at Tojo, he said, "We have the proof right there. Shit, how can we win the war if we don't kill the enemy." The subject was dropped.

As we glided through the quiescent waters with the greatest danger behind us, I experienced a period of comparative relaxation. My thoughts turned to my parents and my siblings, who, with the exception of my brother Martin, were halfway across the earth from me. This war was not easy for our people back home. They could, to some extent, imagine the situations war placed the fighting men in. To some degree they had to have constant concern and worry for us. My mother was a sensitive person who must have suffered greatly since the early days of the war.

It was a time to ponder and evaluate the past weeks and days. One of the 28 ships sunk was a Japanese submarine. It was a victim of the *Skate's* torpedoes. One of the men aboard the *Skate* was Chad McCracken, from my hometown. His father was the school superintendent. Chad graduated from high school one year earlier than I and entered the Navy soon after graduation. It was unusual for two of us from a town of approximately 1,000 people to be in this unique branch of the Navy, and a greater coincidence that we were both on this special war patrol. I thought about Chad and tried to imagine how he was reacting to the recent experiences.

More pressing on my mind during this period of

calm water and semi-relaxation were thoughts of the *Bonefish*. These were disconcerting thoughts which dampened the success of our feat. The *Bonefish* was somewhere on the bottom in the deep water of the Toyama Wan (Bay). As with so many of the submarines lost during this war, there would be no confirmation of her loss; the word would spread throughout our submarine fleet and we submariners would know her fate. But she would be listed as "overdue and presumed to be lost during action against the enemy." And the telegrams from the Navy Department mailed to the next of kin would read "overdue and presumed lost." And the loved ones would cling to the "presumed lost." And they would anguish, but they would hope: "perhaps the *Bonefish* was disabled and captured; if so, the crew will be returned after the war ends." And the sadness, and the hope, and the praying, and the period of waiting would continue.

The sea remained calm. My mind continued to wander and my thoughts turned to my friend who was on the *Bonefish*. He was a country boy from West Virginia. I remember him only as John. He was a member of the forward room crew on that boat, just as I was on the *Flying Fish*. Very likely he was in that torpedo room when the depth charge attack came.

Assuming that they had just sunk a ship, there would have been the usual brief period of elation, and then the preparation for a depth charge attack. I visualized a destroyer, or perhaps two, spray flying as they rushed to the spot where they hoped the *Bonefish* would be. It is possible that a lookout had spotted the periscope or the torpedo wakes early in its path. If so, the Japanese could have zeroed in on the near-exact location.

With a destroyer on either side of the detection

spot, both hurling depth charges in a near overlapping pattern even before trying to make sonar contact, hoping to reach the submarine before she was fully prepared, they had to feel confident.

I visualized some members of the crew on the *Bonefish* working feverishly to get their boat down to 300 feet and to get it stabilized; others rigging for depth charge attack and silent running. I could almost see the first of the depth charges exploding even before the boat began to level off, the men on the bow and stern planes straining with herculean effort, turning the powerless wheels to the maximum up-angle, trying to achieve a level bubble, the exploding depth charges driving the bow deeper, increasing the down-angle of the *Bonefish*.

Next would come the disturbingly clear sonar pinging of the enemy as they electronically scanned that area of the waters, indicating they had the *Bonefish* located. The enemy above would set the depth charges for deeper explosion. The sharp sonar pinging, sounding like a hammer striking the hull, would give them the submarine's exact location. The pinging sound, heard clearly within the *Bonefish*, would be drowned out by propeller noise, the propeller noise increasing in volume and tempo as the enemy rushed away from the target area, and from the explosives which had been dropped.

Directly below in the *Bonefish*, the men would wait in silence. The enemy had released the depth charges directly above them, and the deadly charges slowly sank, reaching for their target. The *Bonefish* crew would hear a sharp click as the pressure mechanism released, allowing the firing pin to strike the detonator. (This sound comes a fraction of a second before the actual explosion. The click is dreaded, hearing it means that the depth charge is very near.) The exploding depth charges would not be isolated explosions, but a series in an almost constant roar.

I visualized the air instantly filling with particles of insulation cork, and glass from some gauges and lights shattering; men hurled against unyielding objects, sustaining injuries. The boat's electrical system could be shorted out, leaving the crew in total darkness, the absoluteness of which is experienced only by submariners. Soon electricians guided by flashlights would be rushing to restore power to the lights.

Now, more depth charge explosions would come, and the bow angle becoming steeper. Water would be blown from the bow area ballast tanks and speed increased to make the bow and stern planes more effective in an attempt to correct the gradual downward slide, but not producing the needed life-saving results. As a last resort and in total desperation, the propellers would be reversed. This noise, created in the attempts to stem the downward movement, would give the enemy an exact fix on their target. The *Bonefish*, not responding to that or any effort to correct her buoyancy, would now be well beyond the depth she was designed for.

The boat's interior, a shambles with broken glass and insulation strewn about, leaking hydraulic oil and spraying water, making rapid movement nearly impossible on the slanted deck. Water under dangerously high pressure would be streaming across compartments and striking the opposite bulkheads. Some of the crew standing on the slippery, slanting deck would be working feverishly to stop the major water leaks. High pressure air leaks, hissing like giant serpents, would be ignored. The *Bonefish* still not

Chapter 19

Home Port Welcome

It was almost as if the waters of the Okhotsk and Bering Seas had extended their paths of liquid tranquillity across the entire Pacific, with the morning's sun reflecting from the water's surface and glistening like a pathway guiding us homeward.

Commander Risser, realizing the possibility that his crew could unintentionally relax and leave the boat vulnerable in case of an emergency, cautioned us via the intercom system. There could be danger lurking from below or above. His brief speech was something like this, "Well done, men. You did as well or better than any captain could expect. We still have many torpedoes left, torpedoes we had hoped to find targets for. There is still a possibility that we could encounter the enemy. Stay alert as we work our way back to Pearl Harbor."

We were not actually hunting and the probability of encountering a target was small. We submariners were putting ourselves out of business. Most of the major Japanese ships, both war and merchant, were on the ocean's bottom. But as always, there was the danger from an enemy submarine, and even more likely, an enemy plane. We did not know that most of their submarines had also been destroyed — most of these by our anti-submarine vessels, our destroyers.

Although the operational activities on the *Flying Fish* did not appreciably change and alertness prevailed, the general feeling and attitude had changed significantly from the time we entered the minefield on June 4, 20 days ago. Now the demeanor of our boat's crew matched that of the water around us. We were heading home! Even Tojo's attitude seemed to change. Perhaps it reflected that of his captors in the forward torpedo room. He became more communicative when he was not working on the torpedo tubes or his writing.

We did not leave our emotional experiences behind in the Sea of Japan. Tojo was there as a constant reminder, and the memories were still vivid. I reminded myself that what we did would actually save lives in the long run. The philosophy of sacrificing a few to save many seemed to apply. Unfortunately, the *Bonefish* was part of the sacrifice.

The homeward voyage was uneventful, as if to match the sea, which remained calm with the weather clear. "Like being home, sitting on the front porch," as Evans expressed it. Each of the submarines took a separate but direct course to Midway Island.

As we approached the dock, the greeting was brief, with none of the pageantry we had received at Pearl Harbor on our return from the previous war patrol. This was to be a brief stop. Our main port would be Pearl Harbor. Perhaps that was just as well, because our docking was not one which any deck officer would want as a prelude to any celebration.

I had the forward room maneuvering watch. The earphones carried every maneuvering command to me and all others who had similar duty. I don't know who the maneuvering officer was, but it probably was not the captain. As was true of all men on the boat, officers were constantly working towards advancement. Their ultimate goal was command of a submarine. After proving docking ability under strict supervision, the officer was, on occasion, given sole responsibility for docking.

We were making a head-on approach into a slip with the main dock directly in front, and extended docks on either side of our entry. This can be tricky because there is no chance to veer off if things are not going well.

From the information coming through the earphones, all seemed to be going normally as we approached the dock in front of us. The commands were, "All ahead one-third." "All stop." A few seconds' pause and then, "All back one-third." Almost immediately, and in a voice sounding concerned, "All back full!" Then, without a pause, "All back emergency!" Just as it takes time to shift an automobile transmission from forward drive to reverse, similar things must be done in proper sequence on a ship. In addition, even after the propellers begin their effort to command the boat's motion, they must overcome the inertia of the extremely heavy vessel. Moments after the last command, the bow made contact with the dock. The point of contact was about 40 feet away from me, and the sounds of crunching came through the hull clearly. The sound continued for what seemed an eternity, but in reality was for a few seconds. Finally the propeller sounds, and the shudder of the boat associated with the "all back emergency speed," came through. Even then, the crunching continued for a moment until the reverse pull of the propellers gained control. The "All stop" was given and we secured from maneuvering watch.

I went topside to view a dock damaged about eight feet in, and our boat's bow sporting a new streamlined design. In defense of the officer who had the docking responsibility, it was evident that he was tricked by an unusually strong current. Docking any ship in tight quarters is always a challenge.

Soon after docking at Midway, the *Flying Fish*, *Tunny* and *Skate* turned their prisoners over to the shore authorities. The *Tunny* rescued a Japanese sailor from a floating crate. His ship was a victim of the *Bonefish* — perhaps the very sinking which triggered the destruction of the *Bonefish*. The *Skate's* prisoners, three in number, came on board the *Skate* voluntarily from a lifeboat containing a dozen survivors from one of the freighters she sank.

The prisoner transfer was almost amusing. After the prisoners were ushered across the gangplank by sailors from the respective submarines, they were met on the dock by an armed Marine Guard, who before transporting them, placed leg irons and handcuffs on them. This was a standard procedure and recognized as necessary precaution, but to those of us who had lived with Tojo, it all seemed too dramatic.

Matt, who from the very first day Tojo came aboard, viewed him with suspicion, and thought he understood more English than he let us know, said, "When that interrogation team puts the pressure on that Jap, he's going to give them a lot of information. That guy's a pretty smart man, and since he's been in their army a long time, he must have some worthwhile information."

Tojo's letter was turned over to the base authorities and was quickly translated. Before we left Midway we received a copy of the translation. It was addressed: Captain, Officers and Men of the ship.

Actually he had little contact with anyone except those of us in the forward room. The letter was lengthy. He thanked us for our kindness. He wrote of feeling guilty about being alive, knowing that all his comrades had perished. He wrote about how he agonized during the time we were sinking his country's vessels and later during the depth charge attack, how he had hoped we would all die. He felt that would have ended his disgrace. His greatest concern seemed to be that we had used him to maintain the weapons which were used against his people. He had no way of knowing, but his work on the tubes had no relationship to their proper function.

During our docking at Midway, one of our ship's signalmen painted a battle flag on our boat's conning tower. The battle flag consisted of our ship's logo, a warlike flying fish leaping from the water with a torpedo in its mouth, surrounded by various flags representing the boat's war record to date. Separate and distinctive small flags indicated three warships sunk, three warships damaged, 15 merchant vessels sunk, nine damaged, nine small craft sunk and three damaged. The small craft were all victims of gunfire, vessels usually not worthy of expensive torpedo expenditure. The barges so recently destroyed weren't worthy of recognition.

Our stay at Midway was brief. We took on some fuel and departed for Pearl Harbor on that same day, June 30. We would enter port flaunting our successful war patrol. To get credit for a successful patrol, the submarine captain's report was accepted at face value. Documented proof that a vessel or vessels representing required tonnage had been sunk, was not required. However, our skipper usually tried to verify his sinkings by photograph, usually taken through

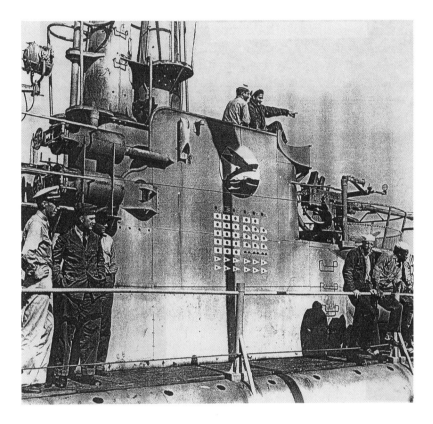

The Battle Flag — indicating warships, merchant ships and vessels of lesser importance credited to the Flying Fish.

the periscope, or by corroboration of another observer.

With a broom attached to our conning tower shear, indicating the successful patrol run, we approached the dock to the sound of band music. The dock was lined with men, and their jubilant greeting was genuine. Unknown to us at the time, unlike most war patrols, some information concerning this one was leaked to the general public about the time we left Midway Island. This was a morale booster for our side and a demonstration of disdain for the enemy. As the war's intensity increased, the American casualty count increased. Our people needed a morale booster. Also, the completed war patrol stood out above any previous submarine accomplishment. For the first time during the war, submarines were receiving public recognition. The conning tower painting depicting the war record of the *Flying Fish* drew considerable attention.

To me, the usual mail call, greetings and fresh foods did not ring with the excitement I previously experienced, even though the dock-side enthusiasm was above and beyond the average. We had not been at sea as long as we had been during the previous patrol, so the craving for fresh foods was not as great. Usually a special treat, the ice cream wasn't all that welcomed. While in dry dock prior to this war patrol, we had an ice cream machine installed. Our ship's cook often served ice cream as dessert. Perhaps I was growing war-hardened, or perhaps the effect of the war patrol was just setting in. Most important and anticipated was the rest and recuperation period awaiting us in Honolulu.

Soon after war had been declared, war-weary submariners began coming back to Pearl Harbor. The

Royal Hawaiian Hotel, considered tops in luxury, was designated exclusively, as a rest and recuperation center for submariners. It continued to be reserved strictly for submariners throughout the war years.

After docking, one-third of the crew was granted liberty. They headed for the hotel and a night on shore. I was among the two-thirds unlucky enough to draw duty. As Matt, who also remained on board, put it, "Hell-of-a way to spend the Fourth of July." Only then did I realize it was Independence Day. After a long 16 hours on the docked boat, we turned her over to a relief crew and boarded a bus. The relief crew and dock workers would take over completely. As was mandated with all returning boats, ours was to be worked over from bow to stern, both inside and outside. When we returned, she would be spick-and-span, and ready for sea duty. We would not see her again until she was ready for taking on weapons and other supplies.

After reaching the hotel, I realized that I had left my wristwatch on my bunk. I moved into my room, then returned to the *Flying Fish*. I had been on shore long enough to clear my nostrils of all the boat's odors and was met by a very obvious and disagreeable stench at the hatch entrance. Disagreeable odors coming from a submarine which had been on a war patrol were the usual thing, and were not new to me. During my relief crew duty, I had been on boats soon after they returned from war patrol. With limited fresh air circulating, the accumulation of various odors trapped in the relatively small interior grew into a massive stench. However, the odor coming from the interior of the *Flying Fish* was difficult to accept. While constantly living in the odor-polluted air, we didn't recognize it as such. Quickly, I retrieved my wristwatch and returned to the hotel.

There were not many of our crew in the hotel when I returned. Even the unlucky last-duty crew had showered, dressed in their best, and headed for lunch and some exciting city activities. The early arrivals made preparations for a long stay. Either through money provided from our boat's recreation fund or courtesy of the Pearl Harbor Base, one room was designated "Refreshment Room." The bathtub, half full of ice, was stocked with a variety of beverages. The beverages included everything from several non-alcoholic types to as many or more of the alcoholic variety. Even torpedo juice, or as Matt called it, "The rabbit-smack'um-knock'em-bear-down stuff," was included.

With the many attractions, the refreshment room was generally ignored. The Royal Hawaiian Hotel is located on Waikiki Beach, and surfboards came with the lodging. It was like having a private beach, very few people used it. It may not have been open to the civilian population. The beach was my favorite area for relaxation, but I did not ignore the city or the surrounding country with its abounding beauty.

The *Skate's* crew was quartered on the floor above us and several days passed before Chad McCracken and I got together to tour the town. We talked about the news from home as we shared bits of information our letters provided. Then the conversation turned to the Sea of Japan patrol.

I was especially curious about Chad's feelings when the *Skate* sank the Japanese submarine. It wasn't until after a few beers relaxed inhibitions that Chad verbalized his feelings about the sinking. Obvious emotion showed through as he related the event. To a degree, I lived the experience with him. That submarine, in a strange sort of way, was one of our kind. A vessel loaded with explosives, which, upon explosion of the *Skate's* torpedoes, was destroyed instantly, without doubt killing all who served on her.

During the second day of our return, each of the submarine Captains was interviewed by a reporter from the *Honolulu Star-Bulletin*. With the exceptions of more minor leaks, the story was held until the war's end. When it was published, it was slightly inaccurate, but the basic facts were there. The following is a portion of that article, with special attention given that section referring directly to the *Flying Fish*.

PEARL HARBOR, July 7 (delayed)—The Sea of Japan no longer has a "private property" sign on it. It is now part of the extensive hunting grounds of United States submarines.

Commanders of eight U.S. submarines related today how they took their vessels into more than a dozen ports of Japan and Korea, sank at least 50 vessels and roamed the Japan Sea almost without opposition.

Cmdr. Risser of the Flying Fish reported that his men were a little worried about how they were going to get in and out of the Sea of Japan. Once in, however, they referred to the sea as the bathtub and enjoyed the sport of sinking small sailing boats loaded with bricks.

"We'd hit one," the commander said, "and he'd start to go down, then just like a dump truck, he'd dump his bricks and come bobbing up again. Most of the boys have a brick or two for souvenirs."

He also told of parking offshore waiting for a tug

and a couple of barges to pass. Instead of passing they began to unload boulders.

"They were evidently building a breakwater," he said, *"and it looked for a minute or two like they were going to start building it on top of us."*

Days passed and scuttlebutt had the *Flying Fish* being converted into a gunboat. If so, what would be our next venture? Near the end of the third week, our stay at the hotel ended. We had enjoyed three weeks of rest and recuperation. A return to a newly-painted and fresh-looking boat usually made it nearly impossible to identify her, if the choice of other submarines was given. Not this time. Despite the choice of several others in the immediate vicinity, the *Flying Fish* stood out. In the short time she was worked on, much had been done. She now sported two five-inch guns, a twin 40-mm gun and the single barreled 40-mm gun which she previously had. She was also equipped with a rudimentary, computer-controlled firing system for the five-inch guns.

Pete and I crossed over the gangplank at the same time. We went directly to the nearest five-incher for a close look and then went to the twin-40, which we assumed would be "our" gun. Pete's hand passed over the twin barrels of the gun, he shook his head, "Can you imagine what we would have done to that tug with this baby? No doubt about it, she's been turned into a gunboat. After all those torpedo misses on the last two runs, I guess the Old Man figured he'd better go to something more reliable." There was a ring in his voice which could have been enthusiasm or concern. I read it as concern. Pete was a rather conservative person, too war-wise and experienced for rash thoughts.

Using a submarine as a gunboat was greatly compounding the danger of submarine warfare.

The *Flying Fish* was now a gunboat. What would be her, our, next assignment? Whatever it would be, most of us were expecting another war patrol in the Sea of Japan.

The Flying Fish as a gunboat prepared for War Patrol 13

Chapter 20

Anxiety and Ecstasy

We returned to our freshly-painted and clean-smelling home, with all the "housework" done, mattress covers replaced, and other minor details completed. It was, as Evans said, "Like moving into a hotel room. Everything done, except that they didn't lay any bath towels out."

Once again, we prepared for war. Trial runs and test dives were made before the boat was loaded with weapons and supplies. Ready for action, we did some target practice on a towed target. As we had expected, Pete and I manned the twin 40-millimeter gun. We agreed that it was a very formidable and extremely destructive weapon.

There was still no word on what our destination would be, but common sense pointed our thoughts to the Sea of Japan. The Japanese Empire, and the people under its rule, needed more softening up as the possible invasion, the final push to end the war drew near.

On August 1, 1945, the *Flying Fish* and eight other submarines moved out by different routes. The *Bonefish* had been replaced. Destination and purpose, repeat strategies: sink, shoot, raise whatever hell possible. In general, try to terrorize the entire nation of Japan.

Things did not seem the same. The changing world events, as written up by the newspaper reporters, gave evidence that Japan was quickly being backed into the land surrounding the Sea of Japan. Still, they continued to fight on even with odds against them increasing. Back in April of 1944, the Soviet Union informed the Japanese that the neutrality pact between the two nations would not be renewed. The Japanese had to know that the Soviets would eventually enter the war opposing them. Past history, the Soviet Union's loss of territorial rights, as well as her defeat in the Russo-Japanese War of 1904-05 were not acts of endearment. With The United States and the British urging the Soviets to declare war on Japan, it was just a matter of time before she did.

This planned war patrol did not invoke the same feeling as the other two had. I wondered if it was all that necessary for us to go back to that sea to cause more destruction and to kill. But, to some degree, the familiar stirring of reckless and youthful enthusiasm for adventure was again awakened within me. We had the enemy on the run. If we, with this patrol, in some way could shortened the war by even one day, we could save lives. Possibly the life of one of my brothers or a hometown neighbor.

In the forward room, there was much discussion about the war patrol upon which we were embarking. This would be the 13th war patrol for the *Flying Fish*. I don't think that submariners are a superstitious lot (some authors have written that they are), but the number 13 did come up during conversation. If any of us had been seriously concerned about that number, we could have asked for a transfer off the boat, and no doubt would have gotten it. Most of the discussion centered around our guns. As Bennett put it, "Just enough firepower to get us in one hell-of-a-lot of trouble. I guess if we need to shoot our way out of the Sea of Japan, we'll be damn glad we have those extra guns. Who knows what kind of hell we'll have to shoot our way through before we get out of there?"

Matt, who had received special training, was assigned the important responsibility as Chief of the Boat. He was preparing to move into the chief's quarters. As he emptied his locker, he nodded in agreement with Bennett and added, "We're going to raise hell in some of those harbors. And if the Japs get wise to our exit, the guns on our gunboats may save our hides." (One of the other boats had been converted into a gunboat, and was equipped with the same type of firepower we carried.)

The train, came to mind; the one which had received considerable thought during our previous patrol, and I used the opportunity to see what response I could get out of Matt. "Matt, now we'll probably shoot that train to pieces with our five-inchers. We won't get a chance to set explosive charges under it. Not that it should matter to you. You wouldn't get to go on such a party anyway, you're too important. As Chief of the Boat you're no longer expendable."

Grinning, Matt said, "You couldn't do anything like that without me. Without me along to take care of you, you'd get your ass shot off."

Despite the seeming lightness of our conversation, all of us must have viewed this patrol as being more dangerous than our previous one. At one point, Canaday expressed the thought that our exit route had to be known to the Japanese. That thought hung heavier than the minefield entry. The *Flying Fish* and the other gunboat, having the greatest firepower, would draw the most counter-fire. But all that thinking was premature — before that, we had the minefield passage and several weeks inside the sea, dealing with enemy planes and escorts. The chances of some of our boats joining the *Bonefish* were high.

The general attitude within the *Flying Fish* was not the same as it was at the beginning of the two previous war patrols. Normally, thoughts which hinged on negativism were seldom spoken. With the war winding down, submarine activity seemed to pick up. Targets continued to decrease in number and submariners had to be even more daring, thus increasing the danger. Now, bits of conversation gave evidence that there was much concern about a safe return.

It seemed that our total thoughts no longer centered around the *Flying Fish*. Other responsibilities and loyalties were coming into play. The G.I. Bill, now a law, commanded a leading role in much of our thinking. With it promising paid tuition, many of us who had given college no previous thought began to think about the war's end and a new life. I had just completed and submitted the required work on two correspondence courses in which I was enrolled. I had ample time, while at sea, to do the course work and the introduction to college academics was interesting, but my purpose was not yet defined. The courses were taken with a "just in case" attitude.

As we proceeded towards the Sea of Japan, the demeanor changed. Thoughts of the war's end and home were pushed aside. The dangers ahead had to be dealt with. This was still a time of war and wars have no future, only the present and a grisly past.

After a few days at sea, we settled into a smooth routine and became full-time warriors again. Almost as if to prepare ourselves, we talked in hopes of sighting some really worthwhile targets. There was much discussion about what we would do inside Seishin Harbor. In addition to anchored ships, the nearby factories and dock facilities were there as gun targets. If we chose the right time, we could destroy some of the trains. I didn't enter into much of that conversation — Pete and I would be up there on the 40-millimeter gun and exposed to everything from ship's deck guns to rifle fire, with the possibility of shore battery fire. I wasn't looking forward to any of it.

On August 6, at 8:15 A.M., the first atomic bomb was dropped on Hiroshima. This city, the seventh largest in Japan, was a rail center and regional headquarters for the Japanese Army. It was virtually untouched by the wrath of America until that hour. With word of the bombing, we were ordered to reduce speed and continue on our present course. We stayed alert, but more or less killed time to see what the outcome would be. None of us knew the true power of the new bomb. Word reached us that it had devastating effects and should force a Japanese surrender.

With our slow speed, we hadn't progressed very far in the three-day period between the two atomic bomb drops, and were still a considerable distance from the Tsushima Strait on August 9. On that day the second target, the historic seaport of Nagasaki, was bombed. Surely now Japan would surrender — and it wasn't long before she did.

Soon after the surrender, orders came to return to a home port. With cheers ringing throughout the boat, we headed west. We turned away from the Land

Chapter 21

Beyond the War

I left home a naive teenage country boy, and returned as an unsophisticated adult warrior. Two and one-half years in the Navy, most of which was served on the *Flying Fish*, had changed me. My brief adult life had centered around the *Flying Fish* and her crew. All of that was to come to an abrupt end. What then? Still living in the familiar quarters of the *Flying Fish*, which was tied up near the New London, Connecticut, Submarine Base, I asked that my discharge time be extended three weeks. I was reluctant to go home, and considered remaining in the Navy. Many changes had occurred in America. How would I fit in? Unlike the situation of the older members of our crew, my future seemed in a state of absolute confusion. They were men in their twenties when they became members of our Navy; men who had left the civilian work force, and jobs they could go back to. (Our government had decreed that all returning veterans must be allowed to return to their previous jobs.) My future seemed in a state of absolute confusion. Although most veterans would not return to those jobs, the knowledge of that promise gave them a mental anchor of stability. There would not be a job waiting

191

for me, or for any of us who went into military service directly from high school.

There was the government-paid tuition for those of us who chose to enter college or any other type of accredited training program. I had been awarded high grades on the two college courses I took through correspondence, but the work on those courses was done at sea when I had unlimited time for their completion. And it was done before I had to make any decisions about the war's end, which seemed a long way off at that time. Could I fit into a formal college program?

It would be difficult to leave the *Flying Fish*, my present home. But then, things on the *Flying Fish* were rapidly changing. Commander Bob Risser was promoted to the rank of Captain and was transferred, and our boat had a new skipper. Evans and Stretch left for home. Bennett and Pappy were married, happy, and homeward bound. Pete and Half Hitch, who would remain in the Navy for a time, were also married and spending their nights on shore with their wives. The feeling of cohesiveness and camaraderie was not the same. The many new crew members just didn't fit in yet. Since there were so many of them, it would take time for integrating the new with the old.

I bought a used automobile, a 1939 Ford sedan, with a badly-damaged engine. Pete helped me, and we did a lot of repair work on it. Satisfied with the condition of the car, and with the three-week extension ended, I left my wartime home. As I left my boat for the last time, I wondered, "What will become of this proud, grand old lady, now that the war is over? War and the destruction of enemy ships is all that she knows."

I drove home, not knowing what to expect. I didn't

receive any hero's welcome. The greetings were not as enthusiastic as when I came home during a brief leave. The fact that I was behind my normal discharge time put me past the jubilant greetings which most servicemen received. Most people just wanted to put the war behind them. They were tired of greeting returning war veterans, there were so many of us.

My family had changed. All my siblings had left home. My parents had relocated and were now living in another part of town. Lion, my faithful old dog, had died. All my friends were gone. Except for two who were war casualties, they had all been home earlier, and were now off in the large cities, earning a living or doing what they had to do. They had their own war demons to deal with. I felt like a stranger in my own hometown. Although I did not have a specific profession in mind, I applied for entrance at three colleges. I felt that I could make a career choice after the first year of basic subjects was behind me. The three colleges to which I made application had closed enrollment. With the G.I. Bill assistance program, the returning veterans were flocking into schools. What to do? The demons of war were still there. I needed some direction but I didn't know which way to point myself. What to do?

Some veterans turned to family, friends, church, or the bottle. One of my high school classmates turned to the bottle and then turned a gun on himself. There were no programs for returning ex-servicemen, where the demons could be put to rest. After the initial fanfare, there was little sympathy for the returnees. Besides, many of the former warriors did not behave as expected. They did not conform. Why should society be concerned with them? Our country was prospering. With prosperity, an over-exuberant, post-war attitude of celebration brought trouble, so more policemen were hired and the jails were expanded. There were means for handling those who did not conform. Most of the nonconformists were war veterans who were fighting the memories within. There wasn't much compassion for them.

So many changes had taken place in America during the war years. The civilians, the "ruling class" who remained at home and legislated those changes while the war was in progress, did not recognize their impact anymore than they recognized the day-by-day growth of a child. To the veteran who had been away and out of touch, with the exception of a leave or two, these changes were unsettling. When I left home, money was scarce and people were more conservative. Life had a slower tempo and neighbors seemed friendlier. Now everyone seemed to have money coming in and something to do, except the veterans. Was there a place for me in my little town? What to do?

Just months ago, I was in death-dealing combat, a respected and needed warrior, a hero in the eyes of the people back home. I was an active participant, fighting in a war for a just cause; a job of unquestionable importance. I was trusted and had a comfortable feeling about myself and my place in the overall scheme of things. I was not looking into the distant future. A warrior dare not do so, only the present and the immediate future are relevant before, during, and after each military engagement. My life centered around my ship, shipmates, and reasonably comfortable living conditions, with private bunk and locker. My meals were served and there was no need for money; if I didn't have any in my pocket, it was merely a temporary inconvenience. All my basic needs were provided. My value to the Navy assured me that I would be well taken care of in any time of emergency. In the Navy, the present and future were secure, now I had to make a new life for myself. This is not a comfortable task for anyone at anytime, and it is especially difficult for an inexperienced, unprepared person. Although I was by age an adult, my transition years from high school to adulthood were not molded in a normal setting. I was not fully prepared for the adjustment required to become a full-time civilian. I was no longer a sailor. I had to change in mind and in lifestyle; to start building a future in an environment I was unaccustomed to. I began to envy Pete. He re-enlisted and was placed in an officer's training program. (When Pete retired from the Navy he was a Lieutenant Commander.)

I was welcome at home, and there was no doubting my family's support, but I didn't feel comfortable about the state of limbo I was in. I packed my car with a few basic necessities and headed for the wilds of Canada. Why Canada? It just seemed the right place, since it was more primitive than anything near home. I viewed Canada as a new world. I had no maps and no particular place in mind. Without realizing it, I was running away from something, and at the same time, I was searching for a pathway to the future. I was being drawn into the wilderness. The wilderness was to become my "family," "friends," "church" and "bottle" — a shrine of peace and purity.

On the outskirts of Toronto, Canada, I stopped for dinner and met a lovely, considerate young waitress. She took a 72-hour vacation from work and for 72 unforgettable hours, all thoughts of past or future were forgotten. I thank you, lovely lady, you started me on the road to recovery.

With limited directions from a local small-town

fisherman, I drove on a primitive road until the road would no longer permit progress. Much to my surprise and annoyance, another automobile and a tent! The owner of these rather expensive possessions was a Canadian Air Force veteran. We obviously had much in common. After a quick visual appraisal and a brief conversation, he invited me to share a trout dinner which was prepared over an open fire. He had been there for nearly a week but still had a large stock of beer. We talked into the wee hours of the morning. Make that a VERY large stock of beer. Head swimming, I made my way to my sleeping quarters — my automobile. My host headed for his tent.

The following morning, after a hearty breakfast served by my host, we conversed for a while, exchanged addresses and I left. I would search for a more isolated area. I wanted to be alone. I wanted to commune with Mother Nature. As for my new-found friend, we never did make contact again.

I found the ideal spot. A road which was partially overgrown lead me several miles into the wilderness. As I drove into a small clearing at the edge of a stream, a whitetail doe with a half-grown fawn bounded across the clearing and disappeared into the forest. Her freedom from any true sense of responsibility generated a momentary feeling of envy within me. But then, she, like I, was a creature of nature with a predetermined purpose in the overall scheme of things.

The first night, I sat on the bank of the stream without the pleasure of a fire, and enjoyed the solitude. No sound came from the forest surrounding me, but I knew some sounds were there; sounds made by creatures with searching eyes, padded feet, gentle hooves and velvet wings. These creatures were searching for food or mates — to them, the most important things in life: these two things, which were more important than self-preservation, except during moments of imminent danger.

Later that same night, a strong wind developed. It blew with considerable force for several hours and threatened rain, but offered only occasional distant lightning and thunder. For a while, I enjoyed this harsh demonstration of Mother Nature.

Nearby, two trees gave off sounds as they rubbed against each other. At times the sounds were agonized and prolonged. Other times they were angry and harsh. There was little resemblance to the sounds of seas crashing on the bow of a ship, so I don't know why I likened it to the *Flying Fish* fighting her way through a sea driven by savage winds. I was reminded of those times when we had a predetermined schedule designating a given location, and could not enjoy the luxury of diving beneath the turbulent surface. My susceptibility to seasickness and memories associated with it played strongly on my mind. Those were miserable experiences. The storm passed and a pleasant morning greeted me.

On my second day at this isolated location, after an early breakfast of bread, sardines and water, I sat on the stream's bank soaking up the morning sun's rays. The seemingly meager meal was adequate, my taste had not been geared to epicurean desires. Availability of money was not a factor, perhaps thrift was. Submariners received hazardous-duty pay, half again as much as normal navy pay, and I took advantage of that financial bonus. Each month, I had money taken out of my pay for the purchase of a war bond. At war's end it totaled enough for the purchase of a new automobile. I didn't even consider such an expenditure. I wanted to keep the feeling of security and to some degree, of independence those savings gave me.

For the first time since leaving the *Flying Fish*, I felt fully relaxed. The pleasant aroma of the conifers permeated my nostrils and acted like an opiate on my mind. When finally I became aware of this obvious gift of nature, I couldn't help but chuckle. Had my senses been made so dull by the stale air of the *Flying Fish* — by the odors of diesel fuel, cooking, the unwashed bodies, and by air often containing a headache-producing quantity of carbon dioxide? I had sat at the same place on the two previous days; strange, that this was the first time I became fully aware of the natural fragrance. I focused on my surroundings, on nature's offerings, the singing of the birds, the gentle gurgle of the stream, and the occasional splashing sound made by a feeding fish. The sounds blended into a soothing rhapsody. How good it was to be alive!

Thinking back to my recent parting from the Canadian Air Force veteran, it seemed like a long time ago. I had done so little, and yet so much seemed to have happened. A door behind me was closing and a new one in the opposite direction was opening.

But life was not just living, it had to be worth living. I felt a need to become a functional, integral part of what made our country tick. The only good thing about war is that it initiates and accelerates scientific research, which in most cases eventually results in improved life for all people. Opportunities would be there for those who were prepared, and education would be the key to many doors of opportunity. This was a fact I recognized.

I fished, but didn't get all that serious about it. I hiked up and down the stream's bank, enjoying nature's gifts and letting my mind lock in on them. At night, the beauty and serenity of millions of stars seemed to act as an elixir. The lonely cry of a loon on a distant beaver pond and the songs of the frogs were my only company. Nothing else could have better suited my needs.

After three days, my mind felt cleansed and I was getting bored. I felt ready to make the adjustment needed to become part of the civilian world.

As I sat in my usual place on the stream's bank, letting my mind wander, the sharp scolding of a jay in a near-by tree brought me from my state of meditation. I heard the jay saying, "Get up and get going, you're wasting time."

With no packing to do, I simply scattered my fire ashes, turned my car around and headed for my hometown. I had a feeling of indefinable urgency.

Soon after returning home, I was contacted by my former high school science teacher. He had talked with the dean of his alma mater and he informed me that they would accept me even though the semester was already under way. He impressed upon me the fact that I would be entering college nearly three weeks late and would have a lot of catching up to do. As he briefly put it, "It won't be easy, but you can do it." With great apprehension I accepted the challenge. I thank you, Charlie Thall, you helped give my life direction.

Enrolled in what is now Mansfield University, I threw myself into my studies with determination fueled by desire, and by a recognized need. Now I was competing as a civilian against my fellow veterans, and against teenagers fresh from high school. I had a purpose. Fortunately the college was operating on a semester schedule, slightly reducing the significance of my tardy entry. With my goals generally established, I could look beyond the war. For a time, the demons of war could be pushed aside.

As I continued through life in my chosen profession, the brief epoch dealing with the war was buried deeper in the recesses of my mind. There the events lay, for the most part rusting and seemingly waiting, until they were pried loose and brought forward during the writing of this story.

Appendix

With written permission, the quoted material in this appendix is from the *Dictionary of American Naval Fighting Ships*.

"The name, *Flying Fish*, is derived from a number of fishes of tropic and warm temperate seas whose wing-like fins make it possible for them to move some distance through the air.

The first *Flying Fish*, a three-masted schooner, was formerly the New York pilot boat, *Independence*. She was purchased, August 3, 1838 and renamed, *Flying Fish*.

Assigned as a tender in the U.S. Exploring Expedition of 1838-42. On August 19, 1838 the *Flying Fish* sailed with her squadron to visit Madeira and Rio de Janeiro while bound for Tierra del Fuego, where the squadron arrived early in 1839. From this jumping-off point, the squadron made its first cruise towards the Antarctic Continent, which it was to discover later that same year, after surveys among the Pacific islands and a visit to Australia.

After the second penetration of the Antarctic, the squadron rendezvoused in New Zealand in April of 1840 to survey Pacific islands northward towards the

Hawaiians, where the ships were repaired late in the year. *Flying Fish* sailed with *Peacock* to resurvey some of the Samoan Islands: Ellice, Kingmill, and Pescarore, before joining the main body of the squadron on the northwest coast of America in July, 1841. *Flying Fish* made surveys in the Columbia River and around Vancouver, B.C., then proceeded to San Francisco, from which the squadron sailed November 1 for the South Pacific, arriving in the Philippines in mid-January 1841. The *Flying Fish* separated from the other ships to cruise the Sulu Seas, then made a planned rendezvous at Singapore in February. Found unfit for further service, the *Flying Fish* was sold before the squadron sailed for home.

The second *Flying Fish (SS-229)* was launched 9 July, 1941 by Portsmouth Navy Yard; sponsored by Mrs. Husband E. Kimmel, wife of the Commander and Chief, Pacific Fleet; and commissioned 10 December, 1941, Lieutenant Commander Glynn R. Donaho in Command. She was reclassified *AGSS-229* on 29 November, 1950.

Of the *Flying Fish's* 12 war patrols, all save the 11th were designated 'successful'. She is credited with having sunk a total of 58,306 tons of enemy shipping. She received 12 battle stars for World War II service."

(I will not give details of all twelve war patrols made by the *Flying Fish*, as printed in the *Dictionary of American Naval Fighting Ships*, instead, I will let the information I have given on patrols eleven and twelve, represent all of her war patrols.)

"After World War II, the *Flying Fish* returned to New London to become flagship of Commander, Submarine Force, Atlantic Fleet. During the eight years, from her base at New London, the veteran *Flying Fish* conducted reserve training cruises in Long Island and Block Island Sound, exercised off the Virginia Capes, trained men of foreign navies, joined in major operations in the Caribbean, and cruised to Canadian ports. On January, 1951, she completed her tour of duty as flagship, and began to serve the Underwater Sound Laboratory in sonar experiments. On 29 February, 1952, at 1053, *Flying Fish* made submarine history as she dived for the 5,000th time, first American submarine to reach such a record. On board for the event was a distinguished party headed by Secretary of the Navy D. A. Kimball. Placed in commission in reserve 31 December, 1953, *Flying Fish* was decommissioned at New London 28 May, 1954 and was placed on sale for scrapping in 1958. On August 1, 1958 the *Flying Fish* was sold to the North American smelting CO., Wilmington, Del. for the sum of $66,200."

(Just as the name *Flying Fish* was handed down from the gallant and worthy Schooner to *Flying Fish* (*SS 229*), it was again handed down to the nuclear submarine, *Flying Fish* (SSN 673). The *Flying Fish* lives, and continues to roam the seas in the interest of America.)

In Remembrance

"My" *Flying Fish* is gone but
the *Bonefish* is still with us.
She cradles her crew within her
hull in an everlasting embrace
as she lies on the bottom of
Toyama Bay.

She and her crew are protected
by the deep water from storm or
strife which may cause turbulence,
rage, or anxiety above them.

May she and her gallant crew
forever lie undisturbed, in the
sleep of eternal peace.

Bibliography

Alden, John D., *The Fleet Submarine in the U.S. Navy*. Naval Institute Press, Annapolis, Maryland, 1979.

Esposito, Vincent J., Brigadier General (Ret.), *A Concise History of World War II*. Frederick A. Praeger Publishers, New York, N.Y., 1964.

Honolulu Star-Bulletin: Saturday, August 11, 1945, "U.S. Submarines Wreak Havoc In Sea of Japan, Enemy's Front Yard," by Roy Cummings, Star-Bulletin War Correspondent.

Howe, Russell Warren, *The Hunt for Tokyo Rose*. Madison Books, Lanham, Maryland, 1990.

National Geographic Society, *The World. National Geographic Magazine*, Washington, D.C., 1988.

Shigemitsu, Mamoru, *Japan and Her Destiny*. E.P. Dutton and Co., Inc., 1958.

The Encyclopedia Americana. Volumes 15 and 19, Grolier Inc. Danbury, Connecticut, 1993.

U.S. Navy, Chief of Naval Operations, Naval History Division. *History of American Naval Fighting Ships, Volume II.* Washington: Government Printing Office, 1963.

U.S. Navy, Chief of Naval Operations, Naval History Division. Source File, "Ships Folders" and "Miscellaneous Records," (mimeographed, declassified U.S.S. Flying Fish war patrol records).

Index

A

Admiralty Islands 44

B

Beardsley, Ralph C. 147
Bennett, Wilfred A. 10, 37, 44, 53, 54, 57, 62, 66, 89, 100, 101, 102, 118, 141, 142, 144, 149, 187, 192
Bering Sea 164, 171
Birkner, Francis R. 85, 117, 127
Bonefish, USS 111, 159, 160, 167, 168, 169, 170, 172, 174, 185, 188
Borneo 14
Bowfin, USS 95, 159
Brisbane 6, 31, 33, 38, 43, 62, 63
Burke, Julian T. 35, 74, 95
Bush, George H. W. 49

C

Canaday, Gerald B. 84, 85, 93, 100, 103, 113, 114, 141, 143, 165, 187
Celebes 14
Chace 66
Cogswell, USS 74, 76, 86
Crevalle, USS 111, 159

D

Davao 1, 3, 4, 11
Davao Gulf 55, 61, 66
Doheny, Edward 66

E

Emmons, Robert C. 115
Eurayle, USS 44
Evans, Cassel J. 10, 37, 38, 39, 43, 62, 78, 79, 100, 127, 129, 130, 131, 139, 146, 172, 185, 192

209